SpringerBriefs in Business

SpringerBriefs present concise summaries of cutting-edge research and practical applications across a wide spectrum of fields. Featuring compact volumes of 50 to 125 pages, the series covers a range of content from professional to academic. Typical topics might include:

- A timely report of state-of-the art analytical techniques
- A bridge between new research results, as published in journal articles, and a contextual literature review
- A snapshot of a hot or emerging topic
- An in-depth case study or clinical example
- A presentation of core concepts that students must understand in order to make independent contributions

SpringerBriefs in Business showcase emerging theory, empirical research, and practical application in management, finance, entrepreneurship, marketing, operations research, and related fields, from a global author community.

Briefs are characterized by fast, global electronic dissemination, standard publishing contracts, standardized manuscript preparation and formatting guidelines, and expedited production schedules.

Agustin Chevez

The Pilgrim's Guide to the Workplace

Springer

Agustin Chevez
University of Melbourne
Parkville, VIC, Australia

ISSN 2191-5482 ISSN 2191-5490 (electronic)
SpringerBriefs in Business
ISBN 978-981-19-4758-2 ISBN 978-981-19-4759-9 (eBook)
https://doi.org/10.1007/978-981-19-4759-9

© The Author(s) 2022. This book is an open access publication.

Open Access This book is licensed under the terms of the Creative Commons Attribution 4.0 International License (http://creativecommons.org/licenses/by/4.0/), which permits use, sharing, adaptation, distribution and reproduction in any medium or format, as long as you give appropriate credit to the original author(s) and the source, provide a link to the Creative Commons license and indicate if changes were made.

The images or other third party material in this book are included in the book's Creative Commons license, unless indicated otherwise in a credit line to the material. If material is not included in the book's Creative Commons license and your intended use is not permitted by statutory regulation or exceeds the permitted use, you will need to obtain permission directly from the copyright holder.

The use of general descriptive names, registered names, trademarks, service marks, etc. in this publication does not imply, even in the absence of a specific statement, that such names are exempt from the relevant protective laws and regulations and therefore free for general use.

The publisher, the authors, and the editors are safe to assume that the advice and information in this book are believed to be true and accurate at the date of publication. Neither the publisher nor the authors or the editors give a warranty, expressed or implied, with respect to the material contained herein or for any errors or omissions that may have been made. The publisher remains neutral with regard to jurisdictional claims in published maps and institutional affiliations.

This Springer imprint is published by the registered company Springer Nature Singapore Pte Ltd.
The registered company address is: 152 Beach Road, #21-01/04 Gateway East, Singapore 189721, Singapore

Forewords

Writing about work and the workplace from the perspective of a pilgrim leads to an inevitable expansion of what we usually associate with these two topics. Experts from four different fields introduce the book from their own viewpoints: the head of workplace design and delivery at a blue-chip company; an authority of organisation design at a top-ranking business school; the head of research in charge of one of the world's largest datasets of workplace experience; and an explorer awarded with the Order of Australia Medal for his contributions to exploration and business.

*

Pilgrimages and workplace design are not a usual combination, but Agustin makes a case for why they should be. This book reminds us of the potential of thinking about something for longer than we usually do – and when that something is the workplace, it can lead to better places to work and a deeper understanding about ourselves.

For me, this book served as a timely reminder of the beautiful complexity in the design and delivery of workplace environments that attracted me to this industry. Unfortunately, it's often the case that we overlook the many opportunities this complexity has to offer and end up following the certainty of the beaten path.

However, in times when we are faced with ever-changing circumstances in the future of work, the lure of shortcuts should be avoided. The decisions we make now about hybrid-work, and the many other choices we are required to make, will have consequential impact on business outcomes and shape the new reality of work – the stakes are high.

I encourage you to accept Agustin's invitation and join him as a fellow pilgrim. You will come across a rich variety of lessons, or signposts as he calls them, which collectively hold the promise of pointing towards a reimagined workplace.

Victor M. Sanchez, Head of Global Design and Build at **LinkedIn**

*

In this wonderfully personal narrative, Agustin recounts his meditations on work, organisations, and their architectures as he walks from Melbourne to Sydney. During such time, the ideas of Charles Darwin, Albert Camus, and James March rub shoulders with each other – and with some iguanas.

For humanist thinkers on organisations, the great bargain with the Devil was struck when our species discovered specialisation. Instead of everybody doing everything needed to produce a result they could each touch, feel proud of, and celebrate, work was now cut into tasks. Each person would do just one task, over and over again – but getting better at it every time. Welcome efficiency! But goodbye variety, autonomy, accomplishment, meaning, and purpose.

The Great Remote Working shock created by the COVID-19 pandemic has a similar flavour to some. We have all discovered, to our (un?)-pleasant surprise, that a lot more of our work is possible without being physically co-present. Welcome (even more) efficiency! Goodbye social connection, community, and spontaneous togetherness.

But perhaps we can strike a better bargain with the Devil this time. As Agustin points out, isolation and absurdity both have their uses as curators of diversity and novelty, and their offspring: innovation. And as the goldrush into the metaverse begins, one can be sure there will be many experiments in producing social connectedness in the virtual world. Some of them may be successful, and who knows, even interesting.

Ultimately, architects, like organisation designers, are in the business of designing interactions among the people who inhabit the spaces and organisations they, respectively, create. Agustin wants us to reflect about either kind of design with a new objective function in mind: one that tunes social interactions to maximise meaning and purpose.

Wouldn't it be interesting to rethink what we do as designers in this fundamental way?

Prof. Phanish Puranam, Roland Berger Chair Professor of Strategy and Organisation Design at **INSEAD**

*

I've always known Agustin as a workplace enthusiast, adventurer, and deep thinker. Whenever I catch up with him over a quintessentially Melbourne coffee, I know I am up for some thought-provoking ideas.

This book is like one of those coffee catchups, and then some. Agustin will take you along an extreme journey – both in the physical world and through his mind. He will pull you in from the very start with a proposition that is counterintuitive to how we think about innovation in the workplace: could the best ideas stem from solitude? Not one to leave questions unanswered, he walks on his own from Melbourne to Sydney to find out. Soon you'll find yourself wondering where his physical journey (walk) takes him next, and where his thinking expedition (pilgrimage) will take us.

The workplace industry could certainly learn a lot by looking outside its own sector, and Agustin takes this a step further – or more precisely 1,281,772 steps further. Through his unconventional, yet brilliant exploration method, he arrives to 34 'signposts' that summarise the key points he picked up along the way.

I've personally reflected on Signpost 6: *"Boredom can become a useful thinking tool."* As COVID-19 wiped out all travel from my diary, it also took away the boredom experienced in airport lounges and flights. These moments were opportunities of reflection, letting my mind wonder and giving way for new ideas to emerge. In a strange way, I miss that. It has made me realise that I need to design some boredom into my working-from-home routine.

Aided by various experts and an extensive review of the literature, Agustin goes to great lengths to get us closer to where these signposts point. But we should too, individually and collectively, share the responsibility to bring the workplace closer to where they point.

Dr. Peggie Rothe, Chief Insights & Research Officer at **Leesman**

*

Few people these days give themselves the headspace to deeply contemplate what truly matters. It's uncomfortable, and in the end, there is no right or wrong answer. And so, it's easier to stay in a busy routine and skim across the surface of life in the falsehood that we have all the answers and life under control.

In climbing the Seven Summits; skiing to the North Pole, South Pole and across Greenland; and on foot in unexplored Amazon, I have had the privilege of long periods of time in remote big nature, completely disconnected from technology and commercialism. Much of that time was focussed on basic survival and physical movement forward, immersed in the present moment. Arising from those meditations is part of my constantly evolving answer to what truly matters: to explore and express our unique gifts for the benefit of others. To this end, I believe that our role in designing workplaces is to enable the exploration and expression of the unique gifts of each member in our teams.

Through his pilgrimage, Agustin set out to find a better place to work – that's what matters to him. Like all pilgrims, he stepped into and embraced the unknown with the courage that a higher force would lay out the path ahead and take care of him in his quest for answers to deep questions – the journey itself became the reward.

Valuable insights in any field can only be produced when a human with accumulated mastery in that field immerses themselves in deep contemplation. Agustin found his signposts for designing workplaces in such a way.

These signposts are now ours to use and create a workplace that reflects what you believe truly matters, without needing to walk from Melbourne to Sydney.

Paul Hameister, OAM, explorer and property developer

Prologue

This book is for people who yearn to embark on an adventure in diversity of ideas about work and the workplace.

In relocating from Mexico to Australia in 2002, I left behind not only my friends and family but also the ability to call myself a 'capital A' Architect due to country-specific regulations. And so it was that one of the first tasks I embarked on in my newfound home was to complete the lengthy process of re-instating my professional registration in order to legally reclaim my professional moniker.

The process called for local work experience, so I dutifully joined an architectural practice and worked on the design of a hospital. Challenges arose early, not only from designing a complex hospital environment but also from incorporating advancements in technology such as the upgrade of x-ray machines. This seemingly innocuous change triggered numerous modifications including replacing backlit viewing boxes with monitor screens to view the now digital x-ray images.

My employer frequently reminded me that we were running out of hours – in other words, professional fees – to manage the various changes created by the x-ray machines and the many other ones. Importantly, there was no time to think about how the new machines would impact the flow of information and human interactions within the environment. To me, this was a critical question that remained unanswered after we dealt with all the practical project delivery questions, and it stayed with me long after I'd wrapped up my work experience. The conundrum is that practising architecture leaves little time to think about architecture, and vice versa.

It was through this process of satisfying the requirements to register as an architect in Australia that I had an epiphany: I needed to think about architecture, in particular as it relates to work environments. With this realisation, I ticked 'retired' on the architect's registration form and decided to think about the workplace as part of a fulltime PhD, *The evolution of workplace architecture as a consequence of technology development* [1].

I have those x-ray machines to thank for an 'early retirement' and for the research I undertook which answered some of the questions I had about workplace evolution, but which also, unexpectedly, unearthed many more.

I didn't know it at the time – how could I? – but all these events were building up to a pilgrimage in search of more answers about the workplace. All it was needed was a spark, something to kickstart the 905 km walk. That spark occurred in a flight from Sydney to Melbourne where I crossed paths with iguanas from the Galapagos Islands.

It's on that flight, with those iguanas, that this book begins.

Contents

Part I   The Road Less Travelled

1	Iguanas, Isolation, and Ideas	3
2	About This book	7
3	Spoiler Alert	9
4	A Note on COVID-19	11

Part II   The Making of a Pilgrimage

5	Anatomy of a Pilgrimage	17
6	No Pain, No Gain	21
7	My Two Rules	25
8	The Herzog Enigma	27
9	The Idea	31
10	Why, and For Which Charity?	33
11	Having Fun	35

Part III   Sisyphus Goes to Sydney

12	Step One	39
13	Life at 4.6 km/h	41
14	My Backpack	45
15	Award Winning Scones	49
16	The Good, the Bad, and the Ugly	53
17	Rubbish Snakes	57

18	Where Are the Idiots?	61
19	Winds	65
20	The Perfect Day	67
21	The Very Last Step	71
22	Mind Lag	75

Part IV Real Steps, Virtual Pilgrimage

23	Virtual Pilgrimage, Real Pain	81
24	Deconstructing Pilgrimages	85
25	El Camino Sisyphus Style	89
26	Postcard from Pamplona	95
27	66 loops	101

Part V Laying Paths

28	Following Signposts	105
29	Fork on the Road	107
30	The Wisdom of the Locals	109
31	Let's Go!	113
32	Your Armchair Pilgrimage	115
33	On Wilderness, Carnivals, and Foolishness	117
34	The Art of Timing and Balance	123
35	The Trails and Territories of Adversity	127
36	All Roads Lead to Rome	135
37	Getting There	139

Part VI Your Creature

| 38 | My Iguana, Your Creature | 145 |

Acknowledgements ... 147

Appendices ... 149

References ... 153

Part I
The Road Less Travelled

Chapter 1
Iguanas, Isolation, and Ideas

April 2016. 6pm.
30,000 ft above New South Wales.

I am on a peak-hour, return leg flight from Sydney to Melbourne following a full day of meetings with clients where I shared the findings from our latest workplace design research. The conversations were fruitful, with a particular focus on innovation – a popular topic among organisations. We discussed the ways a workplace could help unearth ideas that organisations intuitively know exist in the ranks of their employees but can be awfully hard to uncover.

All around me, passengers mirrored my fatigue, they were talked out, idea-empty and looking forward to getting home; the hallmarks of a homeward-bound work commute. Settling into the hour-long journey ahead, I pulled out my iPad and resumed reading Richard Dawkins' book, *The Magic of Reality* [2]. Struggling to concentrate, I caught myself re-reading the same paragraph over and over until I eventually became immersed in chapter three: *"Why are there so many different kinds of animals?"*

Dawkins explains Darwin's proposition about how the iguanas of the Galapagos Islands came to be. In a nutshell, the geographical barriers between the islands resulted in the evolution of three distinct species of iguanas who were cut off by the sea. In perfect isolation on their own islands these populations never met, so their genes had the opportunity to drift apart as they evolved in different ways to adapt to their environments.

> ...it is mainly separations of this kind that were originally responsible for all the new species that have ever arisen in this planet. [2]

My earlier thoughts on how to design workplaces to promote innovation blended with Darwin's theory in a way that wouldn't leave me. I wondered, what if Melbourne and Sydney were on two different islands in the Galapagos? And rather than iguanas, these imaginary places were inhabited by ideas.

I turned the thought around in my mind as I looked out the window at the darkening landscape below me. I reasoned that if geographical separation is what gave us the diversity of *species*, from frogs to elephants, could the same be said about diversity of *ideas*?

As passengers around me in the packed aeroplane settled into silence and their complimentary wine, my mind was taking me to another destination that dealt with isolation and the hyper-connectivity created by travel. Could the ease of movement between Melbourne and Sydney, LA and San Francisco, or Hong Kong and Shanghai breed the intellectual equivalent of a colony of 'single idea-specie'? A colony in which there are many ideas, but they all originate from the same strand.

Reflecting again on the conversations I had held with clients earlier that day, I thought about their workplace challenges in a vastly different way. Could isolation create the necessary conditions for unique ideas to hatch? And could these diverse ideas lead to unknown innovations in an otherwise increasingly hyper-connected world?

Back on the ground and at home I lay in bed unable to switch off. Hours of sleep were sacrificed imagining a society with wildly diverse ideas, the product of isolation. These ideas were as diverse as the species in our planet, and they were roaming amongst us too.

The fantastical imagery was quite thrilling, and it led me to promise myself that the next time I had an idea I would not email it, talk about it over the phone, or jump into a plane to discuss it with my Sydney-based boss. I would give that idea the opportunity to depart from the main colony of ideas and deliver its elusive innovation. And here's the kicker, I decided I would sit with such an idea for as long as it would take me to walk from Melbourne to Sydney.

I'm confident I'm not the only person who has had bravado and steadfast conviction in the early hours of the morning – when one should be asleep and not hatching crazy plans. But this time I promised myself I would follow through.

Over a strong coffee the next morning, my idea seemed so outrageous I had to laugh and convinced myself it would be best to put all thoughts of iguanas and any accompanying menagerie of animals to rest. I tried to forget all about it.

But my iguana thoughts were as relentless as the organisations searching for innovation. I daydreamt often, imagining myself following through with my promise. Daydreams were a good compromise, an indulgence that didn't interfere with common sense. And they worked for the best part of two years when I finally stopped dreaming, laced up my boots and hit the road to test whether isolation would allow an idea to evolve in a way that infused it with unique DNA.

Open Access This chapter is licensed under the terms of the Creative Commons Attribution 4.0 International License (http://creativecommons.org/licenses/by/4.0/), which permits use, sharing, adaptation, distribution and reproduction in any medium or format, as long as you give appropriate credit to the original author(s) and the source, provide a link to the Creative Commons license and indicate if changes were made.

The images or other third party material in this chapter are included in the chapter's Creative Commons license, unless indicated otherwise in a credit line to the material. If material is not included in the chapter's Creative Commons license and your intended use is not permitted by statutory regulation or exceeds the permitted use, you will need to obtain permission directly from the copyright holder.

Chapter 2
About This book

This is a specific type of book, it is a guidebook; and a guidebook serves two purposes. First, it helps you get somewhere you want to go. Second, it makes you aware of historic events, art, architecture, cuisine, culture, and people of the places you go through. It is unlikely you would find construction details of a building, or the recipe for the dishes you enjoy during your travels in a guidebook. Instead, it succinctly describes how all these elements have come together and combined themselves in the experience of a place.

This guide is the same, but in our case that somewhere is a better place to work. And to understand such a place better, this book focuses on what happens at the intersection of design, management, leadership, and 'humanness'.

Crucially, I wrote this guide as a pilgrim and not a walker. You will read about the lessons that came out of the mind – the place where a pilgrimage happens – and not an account of physical feats of the distance covered by the legs.

I invite you to come along as a fellow pilgrim on a thinking journey to incubate ideas about the workplace.

But why stop at ideas? I will venture a guess that this book may do for you what it has done for me: it changed not only the way I *think* about the workplace, but also what I *do* about it.

To mark our pilgrimage and help us navigate the road ahead, I have created signposts that summarise key points. The big black arrow tells us the direction they are pointing to and makes them hard to miss.

Our first signpost is:

> **1) Exchanging ideas too early and too often hinders their diversity and potential to innovate.**

Some signposts, like this one, may seem counterintuitive because they point in the opposite direction of where we think we want to go. These contrasting ideas require deeper discussion, but in the interest of maintaining the pace and continuity of our pilgrimage I have deferred an in-depth discussion of these tricky signposts to Part V.

Open Access This chapter is licensed under the terms of the Creative Commons Attribution 4.0 International License (http://creativecommons.org/licenses/by/4.0/), which permits use, sharing, adaptation, distribution and reproduction in any medium or format, as long as you give appropriate credit to the original author(s) and the source, provide a link to the Creative Commons license and indicate if changes were made.

The images or other third party material in this chapter are included in the chapter's Creative Commons license, unless indicated otherwise in a credit line to the material. If material is not included in the chapter's Creative Commons license and your intended use is not permitted by statutory regulation or exceeds the permitted use, you will need to obtain permission directly from the copyright holder.

Chapter 3
Spoiler Alert

Not long after I returned from my pilgrimage, I was approached by a publisher requesting an article about isolation in the workplace [3]. It was in response to tragic events that transpired at the remote Bellingshausen Station in Antarctica. The incident involved a researcher allegedly stabbing a colleague for giving away the endings of the books he was reading [4]. One spoiler too many led to the unfortunate stabbing.

Contrary to the popular view that spoilers diminish suspense and impair enjoyment by revealing the end of a story before it begins, it has been found that: "*spoilers may allow readers to organise developments, anticipate the implications of events, and resolve ambiguities that occur in the course of reading*" [5].

And this is why I'm going to reveal the outcome of my pilgrimage now, because what I am about to uncover may be uncomfortable for some and it will most definitely be an idea that benefits from early discussion. So here is the spoiler and second signpost:

> 2) The workplace should promote absurdity.

I admit this is a bold and provocative statement. Especially, because it's hard to imagine a suggestion that would clash more with the assumptions we have used to shape the workplace as a temple to rationality, supporting the relentless worship of optimised production. Yet, my pilgrimage created a different view of work environments – it worked.

Absurdity is a rich, layered concept. To entice you with its potential, let's consider its inconsistency of logic and blatant disregard for the incompatibility between two propositions that cannot both be true. Now, consider the innovation, transformational idea, or whatever term you use to describe a future that you once thought was impossible if those two propositions turn out to be simultaneously true.

Despite its outrageousness, Signpost 2 is firmly grounded in the principle that the best environments to host the ever-evolving concept of work are those which nurture our human qualities. In particular, those which set us apart from machines, artificial intelligence, and every other technology that aims to replace our body and mind. That human quality, I believe, is our ability to be absurd.

Consequently, a key signpost throughout our journey is:

> **3) The workplace should nurture our human traits.**

Open Access This chapter is licensed under the terms of the Creative Commons Attribution 4.0 International License (http://creativecommons.org/licenses/by/4.0/), which permits use, sharing, adaptation, distribution and reproduction in any medium or format, as long as you give appropriate credit to the original author(s) and the source, provide a link to the Creative Commons license and indicate if changes were made.

The images or other third party material in this chapter are included in the chapter's Creative Commons license, unless indicated otherwise in a credit line to the material. If material is not included in the chapter's Creative Commons license and your intended use is not permitted by statutory regulation or exceeds the permitted use, you will need to obtain permission directly from the copyright holder.

Chapter 4
A Note on COVID-19

> *All is well here at home – although I'm dreading the moment when they tell us we must go back to the office. I am really hoping they won't say that we have to.*
>
> *– Extract of conversation with a friend in response to 'How are you?'*

Even though the events in this book took place years before COVID-19 hit the world, the lessons of my pilgrimage take on new relevance and urgency in light of the global pandemic and its aftermath. Writing this book in parallel with the world encountering vast and long-lasting changes caused me to ponder the relevance of where we work.

In particular, I have thought about the soul-searching that organisations and employees have gone through during the pandemic. With my researcher's hat on I asked myself, what does it all mean for the workplace?

The motivation in asking this question is a fundamental desire to address the current crisis and to help shape better places of work – not offices. It is not about seeking reactive answers with a short shelf life, but rather developing a guide that leads us to better work environments. This version of workplaces goes beyond proper sanitisation, physically distanced, and well-ventilated offices. It even goes beyond finding the sweet spot of working from home or the office.

The best version of a reimagined workplace will emerge from revisiting our assumptions about the way we use space to host the ever-evolving notion of work. It is also a pathway which might lead us to a better version of ourselves.

What Makes the Boat Go Faster?
In May of 2020 the Prime Minister of Australia addressed the nation to communicate his path to recovery from the COVID-19 pandemic [6]. The PM recounted a story from a time prior to his ministry when he visited the New Zealand Royal Yacht Squadron, who were defending their hard-won 1995 America's Cup title.

The PM commented on the dilapidated state of their offices, their old chairs and scuffed table – a stark contrast to the luxury and expensive image of yacht racing associated with the America's Cup. His hosts quickly interjected: "in Team New Zealand you only ask one question: what makes the boat go faster?"

The PM conceded the condition of their offices made no difference to the speed of the boat. And it didn't, New Zealand won the 2000 America's Cup.

The PM's speech went on, but I stopped listening, my mind flashed to a time when I was presenting the findings of recently completed workplace research to the executives of a large organisation. The mood was tense with no questions at the end, but there was just one comment. I was told that if they had to work in refurbished shipping containers it wouldn't affect their bottom line.

I was left wondering if their confidence in working from shipping containers was because they were so good at what they did that they could do it anywhere, or that they couldn't see a connection between their workplace and the bottom line.

A subsequent apology brought to the surface the immense pressure the executives were under as the reason of such a blunt comment. But the apology was about the tone, not the message itself. Throughout my career I have been challenged with views related to the impact of workplace on performance, but none were expressed as earnestly as that.

I too have asked myself rhetorically many times, "does it matter where we work?" I will admit my motivation was to build an arsenal of reasons why it actually does matter where we work, even if we are incredibly good at what we do.

I now asked myself honestly, what if it really, really, doesn't matter where we work?

Open Access This chapter is licensed under the terms of the Creative Commons Attribution 4.0 International License (http://creativecommons.org/licenses/by/4.0/), which permits use, sharing, adaptation, distribution and reproduction in any medium or format, as long as you give appropriate credit to the original author(s) and the source, provide a link to the Creative Commons license and indicate if changes were made.

The images or other third party material in this chapter are included in the chapter's Creative Commons license, unless indicated otherwise in a credit line to the material. If material is not included in the chapter's Creative Commons license and your intended use is not permitted by statutory regulation or exceeds the permitted use, you will need to obtain permission directly from the copyright holder.

Part II
The Making of a Pilgrimage

Chapter 5
Anatomy of a Pilgrimage

My GPS diligently tracked the 905 km that I walked between two of Australia's major cities and a pedometer counted each and every humble but persistent act of putting one foot in front of another a total of 1,281,772 times.

The continuous thick line in Fig. 5.1 shows the route I chose for my walk from Melbourne to Sydney.

The names of the towns I stopped in and the places I passed through have been left out to focus on the spurs coming off the walking route. These are pathways of the pilgrimage that appear to sprout out of nowhere; points along the walk that come and go, diverge, converge, connect and separate. They seem abstract, yet at times are almost physical.

I'll give you one example to explain these spurs. On one occasion as I approached the outskirts of a town, I caught up with a man a few metres in front of me walking at a more relaxed pace. As I passed him, I could see from the corner of my eye that he sped up to keep up with me; it was as if he wanted to make sure he was actually seeing what he thought he was seeing.

He seemed puzzled by my two backpacks, walking sticks, boots and overall attire which contrasted with the relaxed, laidback feel of the beachside town I was approaching. By this stage of my journey, I was used to people staring at me, so continued walking.

Eventually he asked:

"Hey, where are you going?"
"Sydney", I replied.
"Fuck me!" he said stopping in his tracks as if the response had stumped him.

I lumbered along and several steps later he asked:

"And where'd you come from?"
"Melbourne" I said over my shoulder.
"Fuck me!" he said again.

Fig. 5.1 Anatomy of a pilgrimage

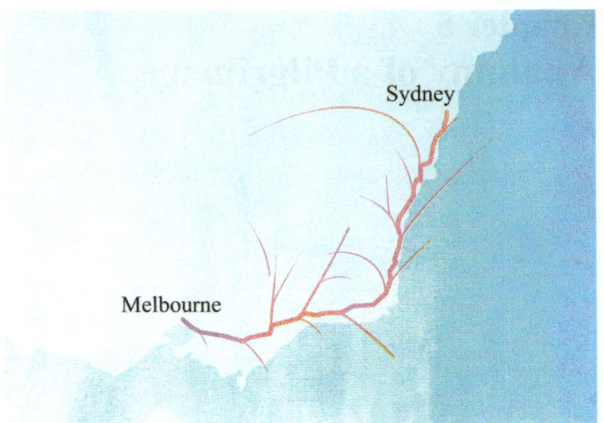

I figured then that I must have been, from a theoretical viewpoint, halfway to where I was going and where I had come from. Ridiculously far from where I started and from where I was going. However, in terms of my physical walk I was entering Narooma, in southern New South Wales, and had already covered about two thirds of the distance from Melbourne to Sydney.

As I walked, I replayed the encounter in my mind swapping my salty-mouthed fellow walker for Zeno, the pre-Socratic Greek philosopher:

> Zeno: "So, Sydney you say? Are you aware that if you are ever to arrive in Sydney you must first walk halfway there?"
> Me: "Yes, Zeno. Catch you later."
> Zeno: "But wait… Are you aware that before you reach the halfway point you must first walk a quarter of the way there?"
> Me: "Yep! And I won't get there by chatting, so…adios amigo."
> Zeno: "No, no, wait! Before you get to a quarter of the way you must have covered one-eighth, before that, one sixteenth and so on..."

He would then pull out a piece of paper and scribble an equation to show me, Fig. 5.2:

> Zeno: "See, you need to arrive at an infinite number of intermediate points, so you will never arrive in Sydney! Travel over any distance can be neither completed nor begun, and so all motion must be an illusion."
> Me: "Fuck me!"

Two millennia after his death, great thinkers are still working on solutions to Zeno's motion paradoxes. It has entertained the minds of Aristoteles, Archimedes and more recently the philosopher, logician and Nobel Laureate, Bertrand Russell [7].

Fig. 5.2 Zeno's scribble. Though the scribble mathematically represents his idea, such notation was not established back then. Zeno didn't speak English, either

The pilgrimage I was on was held together by a particular type of logic. It was not the kind of logic that teaches us to explain what we already know, but to paraphrase Descartes, the kind which allows us to direct our reasoning with a view to discovering truths of which we are ignorant [8].

Open Access This chapter is licensed under the terms of the Creative Commons Attribution 4.0 International License (http://creativecommons.org/licenses/by/4.0/), which permits use, sharing, adaptation, distribution and reproduction in any medium or format, as long as you give appropriate credit to the original author(s) and the source, provide a link to the Creative Commons license and indicate if changes were made.

The images or other third party material in this chapter are included in the chapter's Creative Commons license, unless indicated otherwise in a credit line to the material. If material is not included in the chapter's Creative Commons license and your intended use is not permitted by statutory regulation or exceeds the permitted use, you will need to obtain permission directly from the copyright holder.

Chapter 6
No Pain, No Gain

Having a rule or prescribed manner in which distance should be covered is a common feature among most pilgrimages. Rarely are these intended to improve the comfort or welfare of the pilgrim, in most cases, it's quite the opposite. For example, a Tibetan pilgrimage requires pilgrims to perform body-length prostrations along a rocky path for 50 km – suffering is a necessary part of the journey [9]. Whereas most of us hope to be saved *from* pain, others hope to be saved *through* pain [10].

Though far from Tibet, I still walked through the cold, wet southern Australian winter and felt as though I must have a lot to be saved from the pain I was experiencing. However, my motivation for walking in winter was to avoid the bushfire season and Australia's infamous snakes which are too smart to be out in the cold. The truth is, I had no interest in aligning my walk to the discomforts of a pilgrimage. In fact, I was carrying an inflatable pillow – a testament to how little comfort I was willing to forfeit.

Despite my pillow and many other attempts to maintain comfort, I couldn't dodge discomfort and adversity, and with them came invaluable insights.

In *The 3rd Man* [11] Orson Welles reminds us that during the terror and bloodshed that prevailed in Italy for the 50 years the Borgias ruled, there emerged Michelangelo, Leonardo da Vinci, and The Renaissance. Switzerland, on the other hand, had 500 years of democracy, peace, and brotherly love and has given us the cuckoo clock.

Countless examples exist where challenging circumstances have produced invaluable lessons, fresh thinking, and innovation. You might even have experienced that yourself. Why then, do we seek to avoid adversity so much in the workplace?

Comfort in the workplace is a prolific area of research. A hunt for the optimal lighting, ambient temperature, noise levels and other environmental conditions intended to mostly increase productivity [12]. To this end, it would seem right, even obvious, to aspire to be like Switzerland. Maybe even with some hints of peppermint odour to improve speed and accuracy while typewriting [13]. But what if our desired outcome was more closely aligned to The Renaissance, could adverse environments lead to Renaissance-like innovation?

There is an irony that I hope will not be lost in that after packing a pillow, I am now questioning comfort. And I certainly prefer the smell of peppermint over the flattened and decomposing corpses of the kangaroos littering the roadsides to Sydney. To be clear, I'm not talking about unnecessary adversities in the workplace, but what requires further examination is why we pursue more frictionless cuckoo-clock work environments, when innovation might be better served by exploring the type of adversities worth keeping, and perhaps even introduced in the workplace.

Could *pilgrimising* the workplace lead to Renaissance-like outcomes?

Our next tricky, very tricky, signpost is:

4) Adversities are worth keeping, even introduced, in the workplace to promote innovation.

Explaining the usefulness of adversity is not what makes this signpost problematic. After all, adversity has been recognised as a path to wisdom [14] – even salvation for some. For the record, a study [15] found that those whose work required logic and objectivity in their outputs tended to be more emotionally stable (think Switzerland and the cuckoo clocks) whereas those producing creative outputs had experienced more adversity, such as depression (think Italy during the Borgias and the Renascence). The study points to a 'powerful relation' between adversity and creativity.

We have also been cautioned about the dire consequences of ironing out adversity. Nietzsche warned of the risks of aspiring to a society which seeks comfort and routine as this could breed an apathetic person who is tired of life, takes no risk, and has no dreams [16]. Fortunately, there are people preventing us from meeting such a fate. A team of researchers [17] are reframing the perceptions of risk in outdoor play areas to ensure children benefit from uncertainty and challenges in increasingly risk-averse playgrounds.

What is tricky about Signpost 4 is finding practical ways in which adversity in the workplace can lead to innovation, while recognising that adversity is, well, adverse and we would do well to avoid it despite any benefits it might deliver. This is the trickiest part of our fourth Signpost and the one which points in the opposite direction to how workplace design deals with adversity – and so it will be discussed in Part V.

Open Access This chapter is licensed under the terms of the Creative Commons Attribution 4.0 International License (http://creativecommons.org/licenses/by/4.0/), which permits use, sharing, adaptation, distribution and reproduction in any medium or format, as long as you give appropriate credit to the original author(s) and the source, provide a link to the Creative Commons license and indicate if changes were made.

The images or other third party material in this chapter are included in the chapter's Creative Commons license, unless indicated otherwise in a credit line to the material. If material is not included in the chapter's Creative Commons license and your intended use is not permitted by statutory regulation or exceeds the permitted use, you will need to obtain permission directly from the copyright holder.

Chapter 7
My Two Rules

A pilgrimage needs boundaries, and I defined mine before I took my first step. Rule One was simple and straightforward, I had to be alone. I walked by myself and avoided contact with family or friends so that I could evolve my ideas without the influence of others. For safety reasons, I sent daily text messages to let people know where I was and that I was ok, but that was all I allowed myself.

Rule One did not mean I couldn't converse with people I met along the way. However, speaking to strangers reminded me of how lonely I was and was left feeling isolated. At other times I actually enjoyed the solitude and through this experience became quite aware of the differences between aloneness, solitude, and isolation – an important trilogy shaping work environments.

The ability to work anywhere, anytime has led to the development of organisational structures with the potential to inflict Rule One in a distributed workforce. But working alone doesn't necessarily end in feelings of isolation, just as working with others doesn't eliminate them – an employee working amongst others can still feel isolated if they don't feel part of the group.

When isolation does hit, it can lead to depression, stress, lack of motivation and burnout [18]. The impact of isolation on the reduction in lifespan has been equated to that caused by smoking 15 cigarettes a day [19], a contentious but illustrative equivalence.

Let's return to the tragic incident at the remote station in Antarctica. It wasn't the spoiler, but *cabin fever*, the term used to describe irritability due to prolonged isolation, that was later pinpointed as the likely underlying factor that led to the stabbing. The negative effects of isolation can revoke any benefits associated with solitude. The key thus lies in finding the sweet spot of aloneness, not only for our mental health, but also for the *health* of the idea we seek to incubate through this process.

As a counterbalance to the premise that sent me on my pilgrimage, it has been found that the best outcomes can be achieved by balancing the right amount of one's own ideas with those of others. By analysing over 10 million financial transactions, a team of researchers showed that investors who were in that sweet spot of their own and others' ideas outperformed those in the echo chamber who copied each other's ideas, as well as those who followed only their own ideas [20].

We can summarise the implications of Rule One in the following signpost:

> **5) Aloneness needs to be within the ideal conditions of its effects on us (solitude) and the quality of the idea itself.**

My second, and last rule, was to avoid distraction. No music or podcasts, no books or anything that might help to pass the time. This rule helped to ensure the pilgrimage remained focussed and not a holiday, but its side effect became obvious on day three when the novelty had already worn off and I got bored.

Really, really, *really* bored.

At one point, I couldn't think about anything else other than how bored I was. My boredom was so distracting, it got in the way of the rule's purpose of forcing me to focus. At that point, I could have been bingeing on a TV series or doom-scrolling on my phone – at least then I would have been entertained.

Surprisingly, Rule Two demanded greater effort to follow than Rule One. Well, surprising to me, but not to researchers studying boredom who found that "*many* [of the participants] *preferred to administer electric shocks to themselves instead of being left alone with their thoughts*" [21]. Thankfully, I came out the other side without resorting to electric shocks and when I did, I was able to appreciate boredom. Once transcended, I found boredom beautiful and a useful thinking tool.

Our next signpost:

> **6) Boredom can become a useful thinking tool.**

Open Access This chapter is licensed under the terms of the Creative Commons Attribution 4.0 International License (http://creativecommons.org/licenses/by/4.0/), which permits use, sharing, adaptation, distribution and reproduction in any medium or format, as long as you give appropriate credit to the original author(s) and the source, provide a link to the Creative Commons license and indicate if changes were made.

The images or other third party material in this chapter are included in the chapter's Creative Commons license, unless indicated otherwise in a credit line to the material. If material is not included in the chapter's Creative Commons license and your intended use is not permitted by statutory regulation or exceeds the permitted use, you will need to obtain permission directly from the copyright holder.

Chapter 8
The Herzog Enigma

> *At the end of November 1974, a friend from Paris called and told me that Lotte Eisner was seriously ill and would probably die. I said that this must not be, not at this time… I took a jacket, a compass, and a duffel bag with the necessities… I set off on the most direct route to Paris, in full faith, believing that she would stay alive if I came on foot.* [22]

The renowned German filmmaker Werner Herzog started walking from Munich to Paris in a bitterly cold northern European winter, believing that in doing so he could save his friend and film critic Lotte Eisner. I will not distort what Herzog wrote about so beautifully in his book *Of Walking in Ice* [22] but, for me, the most striking part of his journey remains its spontaneity. True, he had a strong motivation.

Herzog didn't spend long nights reading endless reviews about tents or comparing brands of socks, but I did, and where he wrote, *"where I'm going to sleep doesn't worry me"*, I used Google maps and other sources to plan my nights in advance. His spontaneity made me ponder the 2 years I had taken to embark on my own pilgrimage. Why wasn't I able to 'do a Herzog', the pilgrim's equivalent of Nike's 'Just do it'?

Comparing Herzog's decisive action with my delayed start led to interesting insights that were surprisingly connected to organisational growth. Understanding how organisations grow provides clues into the amount of space they might need in the future, and in 2016, I was given the opportunity to go to the United States to study just that. A key conclusion which came out of that research was that as organisations grow, space needs not only to be bigger to accommodate extra people, but also that space needs to be *different* to help organisations overcome the challenges and capitalise on the opportunities that may come as they go through different growth and maturity stages [23].

The study involved many hours of interviews with people running start-up companies in the US, and once I got back, we did more interviews with similar entrepreneurial types in Australia. The interviews we did left a long-lasting impression on me. In particular, the way in which those we studied brought to life the nuanced difference between *preparedness* and *readiness*. A subtle difference, but an important one that helped me solve my Herzog enigma.

Readiness and preparedness both relate to personal attitudes towards an event. But where readiness is about feeling capable of taking immediate action, preparedness is the degree to which one feels able to deal with the consequence of an event, when or even if it ever happens. The entrepreneurs we met in our study exuded readiness in their willingness to do whatever was required of them to achieve their goals.

To me Herzog was an entrepreneurial pilgrim, while I on the other hand prepared for 2 years and then spent the early part of my pilgrimage feeling more prepared than ready to walk the next day. It was only after several good doses of repeated preparedness that I started to feel ready.

Herzog inspired me to think about preparedness and readiness in terms of execution, literally taking the first step. Mildred Norman who is better known as Peace Pilgrim [24] led me to ponder on what it takes to feel prepared, or ready. Peace Pilgrim walked across the US for 28 years covering more than 40,000 km carrying only a few grams of equipment. In contrast, I needed 15 kg of equipment to feel prepared to walk to Sydney.

If you are also someone who finds it unhelpful to have equipment described by its weight, rather than the purpose of the items themselves (I could have been carrying 15 kg of potatoes) then it's likely you'll share my confusion at the all-too-common practice of benchmarking workplaces by the amount of square metres per employee, rather than understanding how the environment supports the organisation in its journey.

Contrasting my experiences with both Herzog and Peace Pilgrim taught me an important lesson, not only about the difference between preparedness and readiness, but also about their subjectivity. At the outset of planning my walk I meticulously documented the items to be packed and the training required in order to include these details in an appendix for others interested in following a similar path. But you won't find that appendix, I have changed my mind – after all, you would only be reading what it took to make me feel prepared.

However, to save my reputation, Fig. 8.1 shows part of what being prepared looked like for me – no 15 kg of potatoes. As for Peace Pilgrim it was a toothbrush, one set of clothes, a comb, and a pencil.

For the entrepreneurs in our organisational growth research, their list of what was necessary for their organisation also varied. Of relevance to our study was their perceived need of having, or not having, an office. We learnt that it wasn't the number of employees or amount of revenue which would predict whether a start-up company would leave behind a home office or coworking space to move into their own offices.

There were those who move because of newly acquired obligations. For example, becoming a publicly listed company almost always imposes a move to comply with confidentiality of information requirements which has little to do with headcount.

But most start-ups moved into their offices to develop their own identity as an organisation, at remarkably different headcounts.

Fig. 8.1 Getting prepared

Combining the lessons from business and pilgrimage entrepreneurs revealed to me the subjectivity embedded in what we need to satisfy our personal setpoint to make us feel either prepared or ready. The fact that this setpoint varies so greatly in an activity which can be reduced to putting one step in front of the other, highlights the complexities of establishing setpoints for organisations with intrinsically more complex activities. Hence the next signpost:

7) The subjectivity behind preparedness and readiness hinders the benchmarking of workplaces.

I also learnt I don't have an entrepreneurial bone in my body; nevertheless, a lot can be achieved by feeling prepared, including feeling ready… eventually.

Open Access This chapter is licensed under the terms of the Creative Commons Attribution 4.0 International License (http://creativecommons.org/licenses/by/4.0/), which permits use, sharing, adaptation, distribution and reproduction in any medium or format, as long as you give appropriate credit to the original author(s) and the source, provide a link to the Creative Commons license and indicate if changes were made.

The images or other third party material in this chapter are included in the chapter's Creative Commons license, unless indicated otherwise in a credit line to the material. If material is not included in the chapter's Creative Commons license and your intended use is not permitted by statutory regulation or exceeds the permitted use, you will need to obtain permission directly from the copyright holder.

Chapter 9
The Idea

As important as it was to be prepared, I still needed to work on the reason why I needed to be prepared. I needed an idea to incubate. Choosing the right idea was critical, I didn't want to finish the walk only to discover that my mind had figuratively walked in the wrong direction, even if my sore legs made it quite clear they had taken me to Sydney.

With that in mind, I now invite you to think about what topic or idea you would choose to ponder for the duration of almost one thousand kilometres walk. As you do, remember Rules One and Two: you will be alone with your thoughts for as long as it takes you to walk the distance. And you will get bored.

Readers of early drafts of this book shared their ideas and personal introspections. These included pondering on "why I do the things I do?", explore ways of managing conflict between individual and collective behaviour, seek a better relationship with oneself and others, as well as finding the inspiration to write music and pursue hobbies.

If we ever cross paths, I would love to hear what your idea was.

In my case, I wanted to develop an idea about the environments that would support our future working lives. As part of this I would consider *where* we work with a much broader application than just the office of the future. To achieve this, I needed a good understanding of the meaning and nature of work itself, particularly in relation to the much talked about job substitution that cognitive computing is expected to bring [25].

I found the most suitable metaphor for my pilgrimage in the tale of Sisyphus. Who's that? In Greek mythology, Sisyphus was a cunning man best known for the punishment he received from the Greek gods for his many misdemeanours: to push a large boulder up a hill, only for it to roll back down when it reached the top. Then repeat the task over and over, for eternity.

Sisyphus' punishment illustrates the lack of purpose and meaning that can be experienced in various work-related tasks, or with life at large.

At its most basic level, the story of Sisyphus encouraged me to reflect on what might come from doing something as meaningless as putting one foot in front of the other, over and over, for what seemed like an eternity. But more than that, his onerous punishment served as the backdrop to my idea: to find purpose in an era of increasingly automated work, not only in the domains of physical work of assembly lines, but also in cognitive activities of office workers.

Imagine if Sisyphus' boulder was put on a conveyor belt that took it up and down the hill automatically, he might experience some immediate relief, perhaps joy, followed by a well-deserved rest. But then what?

In *The function and meaning of work and the job* [26], a classic study on organisational psychology, the researchers hypothetically removed the economic function of work by creating scenarios in which people didn't need to work for money. Surprisingly, 80% of people in the study said they would still keep working. The study concluded that even if workers had enough money to support themselves, they would still value work in avoiding boredom, keeping ties to society, promoting personal fulfilment, and maintaining a sense of well-being.

The meaning of work has intrigued psychologists, sociologists, economists, and organisational scholars for decades and it has inspired philosophers for centuries [27]. Architects do not tend to appear in such lists; nevertheless, we could design better places to work if we understood their meaning as much as their function.

Consequently, I named my pilgrimage *Sisyphus goes to Sydney* and a new signpost raised:

> **8) Understanding the meaning of the workplace as well as its function can lead to better places of work.**

Open Access This chapter is licensed under the terms of the Creative Commons Attribution 4.0 International License (http://creativecommons.org/licenses/by/4.0/), which permits use, sharing, adaptation, distribution and reproduction in any medium or format, as long as you give appropriate credit to the original author(s) and the source, provide a link to the Creative Commons license and indicate if changes were made.

The images or other third party material in this chapter are included in the chapter's Creative Commons license, unless indicated otherwise in a credit line to the material. If material is not included in the chapter's Creative Commons license and your intended use is not permitted by statutory regulation or exceeds the permitted use, you will need to obtain permission directly from the copyright holder.

Chapter 10
Why, and For Which Charity?

The question I was asked most frequently before, during and after I completed my pilgrimage was: "why?". Sometimes I would give full Galapagos-iguana answers and at others I avoided answering altogether by suggesting "why not?". Without a doubt, the latter was more convincing.

"Why?" was nearly always followed by "which charity are you doing this for?" I didn't have one. The disappointment of my answer reflected an ingrained assumption many have that such an undertaking needs to be carried out in sponsorship of something worthwhile and with social recognition.

Pilgrimages are traditionally done in pursuit of one's own purpose and motivation, not for a charity. Keeping with the tradition, I made the deliberate decision not to have a nominated charity. As it turned out, this decision was an enabling factor that led to the most important outcome of my pilgrimage.

Open Access This chapter is licensed under the terms of the Creative Commons Attribution 4.0 International License (http://creativecommons.org/licenses/by/4.0/), which permits use, sharing, adaptation, distribution and reproduction in any medium or format, as long as you give appropriate credit to the original author(s) and the source, provide a link to the Creative Commons license and indicate if changes were made.

The images or other third party material in this chapter are included in the chapter's Creative Commons license, unless indicated otherwise in a credit line to the material. If material is not included in the chapter's Creative Commons license and your intended use is not permitted by statutory regulation or exceeds the permitted use, you will need to obtain permission directly from the copyright holder.

Chapter 11
Having Fun

Along one of the most popular pilgrimages in the world, *El Camino de Santiago*, in Spain, walkers are greeted with "buen Camino" to wish them a good way both physically and spiritually. My version of buen Camino was an enthusiastic and quintessentially Australian "Have fun!" followed by a wave. I would then wave back with a cheerful "thanks, I will!"

It wasn't fun. Really, not at all.

I was constantly hungry, even while I was eating, and with each day a new pain developed in parts of my body that I didn't know I had. Unfortunately, I did not experience the delayed sense of fun that ultra-marathon runners call Type Two Fun either. These superhuman athletes argue the pain and sense of despair they feel prevents them from having fun at the time, which is what they call Type One Fun – or just fun for the rest of us. But they do experience a retrospective type of fun once their sense of achievement kicks in and have a shower and a good rest. That fun is Type Two Fun.

I'm here to confirm that despite many showers and rest since my walk, fun has yet to make an appearance.

But 'fun' seems to have a shared quality about it, irrespective of how, when, or if it's experienced. Fun can justify doing something as crazy as walking to Sydney – and working long hours. This aspect of fun has been capitalised on by proponents of the 'office-as-playpen' concept which once featured workplaces with colourful beanbags and ping-pong tables. Now, the talesmen of hip, cool and fun places to work are breathtaking digital installations in the lobby, in-house top chefs, games room, and furry babies walking around the office. However, the proposition is still the same: employees would stay put and work hard in a fun environment.

While designing experiences is as ancient as the earliest human impulse to develop rituals and ceremonies [28], the influx of experience designers whose main function is to conceive of unimaginable journeys in the workplace would have been unthinkable a few decades ago. Today, 'experience' is paramount.

However, if these experiences are not anchored back to how employees perform their tasks (division of labour) and how these tasks are then reintegrated (integration of effort) to meet the strategic objectives of their organisation, such embellishments of the workplace might turn out to be just gimmicks [29].

Workplace experiences that are disconnected from how the organisation itself is designed, might be well intended, but as ill-fitting as a 'have fun' is for someone who has been walking all day, feels miserable and hungry.

The resulting signpost:

> **9) Experience design and organisation design need to be aligned in the workplace for the organisation to achieve its objectives.**

This alignment could also help to avoid the workplace becoming a trophy for disciplines whereby those from property and design tether the ever-evolving notion of work to the office, and those in organisation design and information technology aim to free 'work' from it.

Open Access This chapter is licensed under the terms of the Creative Commons Attribution 4.0 International License (http://creativecommons.org/licenses/by/4.0/), which permits use, sharing, adaptation, distribution and reproduction in any medium or format, as long as you give appropriate credit to the original author(s) and the source, provide a link to the Creative Commons license and indicate if changes were made.

The images or other third party material in this chapter are included in the chapter's Creative Commons license, unless indicated otherwise in a credit line to the material. If material is not included in the chapter's Creative Commons license and your intended use is not permitted by statutory regulation or exceeds the permitted use, you will need to obtain permission directly from the copyright holder.

Part III
Sisyphus Goes to Sydney

Chapter 12
Step One

1st July 2018. 6:45am.
Federation Square, Melbourne.

I am both surprised and grateful to see that a handful of friends came to the city for a send-off. It's dark and we make efforts to recognise each other's silhouettes in the blackness, eventually realising that it's too early and cold for anyone besides us to be in the square on such a crisp Sunday morning.

Good wishes are wrapped in small talk, and I show off my backpack with unearned pride. We say our goodbyes and I take my first step. The pace of the first few kilometres is uncomfortable, I rush along as if I am being chased or am following someone walking at a much faster pace. Gradually, I settle into a pleasing, steady rhythm.

The winter sunrise illuminates the day, and the idiocy of the adventure rears its ugly head. I wrestle with an inner dialogue: "tell me again, how walking to Sydney is going to help me uncover answers about work and workplace design?" I complement myself on asking such an excellent question, one that I suddenly could not think of a suitable answer. The pace becomes uncomfortably fast again.

Determined not to waste the next two months of leave from work (it turns out that when thinking about work, one cannot work), I encourage thoughts of purpose, Sisyphus, and the future of work. If your mind has ever gone blank after you have been asked to tell a joke and the awkward silence prompts you to tell the lamest joke that pops into your head, you'll know what happened to me next. I couldn't think, and when I did, my thoughts made me wonder how on Earth I had ever made it to adulthood.

My expectations that the trip be worth the time and effort I was investing cast a cloud on the early days of the pilgrimage. Ironically, it began to be worth it when I stopped trying so hard and relaxed.

I'd barely reached the outskirts of Melbourne when I got asked for the first time "why" and "which charity", followed by the less frequent, but more worrying caution "be careful, there are idiots out there." I had every reason to believe these warnings, they came from people who seemed to have led lives far from cosy desks. If they were worried about idiots, I should be too.

I had not prepared myself for idiots.

Open Access This chapter is licensed under the terms of the Creative Commons Attribution 4.0 International License (http://creativecommons.org/licenses/by/4.0/), which permits use, sharing, adaptation, distribution and reproduction in any medium or format, as long as you give appropriate credit to the original author(s) and the source, provide a link to the Creative Commons license and indicate if changes were made.

The images or other third party material in this chapter are included in the chapter's Creative Commons license, unless indicated otherwise in a credit line to the material. If material is not included in the chapter's Creative Commons license and your intended use is not permitted by statutory regulation or exceeds the permitted use, you will need to obtain permission directly from the copyright holder.

Chapter 13
Life at 4.6 km/h

Before setting out on the walk, I had read books about pilgrimages and the practicalities of long-distance trekking. I got inspiration from the former and good tips from the latter. Hot tip: if your hair stands on end, you should drop on your knees and bend forward, but not lie flat on the floor, because lightning is about to strike you.

I now recall with a smile the many times I nearly initiated the lighting strike sequence after feeling the slightest movement in my scalp on stormy days.

I also read books about sophists, epicureans, and stoics because I thought they might be good company during my pilgrimage. They were.

One text that kept coming into my mind was *Learning from Las Vegas* [30], which I read as an undergraduate student – over 20 years earlier but hadn't thought about it since. The authors present an interesting analysis between the speed a person travels and how they read their environment.

In the crowded, narrow alleyways of a Middle Eastern Bazaar, the authors argue, a person travels at a walking speed of approximately 3 miles per hour (4.8 km/h). The walker can smell, see, and even touch the merchandise on offer. As the speed of the observer increases, objects are replaced by symbols that communicate the message related to the objects they replace. The substitution is necessary because communication no longer occurs in the way it does at slow speeds when we can see an apple or an orange. Moving faster, we need a symbol, the sign of a fruit shop. The size of symbols must increase with the speed of the observer for effective communication to take place.

My overall average speed walking to Sydney was 4.6 km/h, just a fraction below that of the walker in a Bazaar. I experienced life in a slowly changing environment. Yet as I travelled roads that were designed for the faster speeds of cars, objects were generally replaced by symbols. The environment I traversed was clearly designed to be experienced at greater speeds than that of a pilgrim.

As predicted, the symbols for a petrol station were visible long before a bowser came into sight. Travelling just below Bazaar speed, symbols were unnecessary, too big and visible for longer than required. Of the many symbols for petrol stations I saw, one in particular caught my attention, Fig. 13.1.

Fig. 13.1 Petrol station symbol

This bright pink aeroplane with its nose buried firmly in the grass beckoned me to the petrol station. Inside, were the eclectic memorabilia of boxing legends of days gone by and mementoes of singers old enough to have done comeback tours, twice-over. The narrative captured on the walls lived up to the expectations set out front by the pink aeroplane. The aircraft was a symbol of the owner's eccentric personality, there to broadcast identity and not just point to a place to fill the tank of one's car.

I spent an unwarranted amount of time in the eclectic shop considering that I had no car to fill up. But as the time passed, I heard the owner's story and learnt more about the objects he'd collected. The aeroplane cost him AUD$1000, which struck me as both a bargain considering how well it acted as a symbol and also overpriced since it was mostly junk painted pink.

Can we learn a lesson about the workplace from the pink aeroplane? If so, it may be that unless we are running late for a meeting, we move through the office at a Bazaar pace of 4.8 km/h or slower and while we do, we are in close proximity to people. Therefore, one might assume symbols in the workplace are not required.

But my story of the messiest desk I have ever encountered might challenge this assumption. The desk was discovered during a workplace observation, it was buried under piles of paper and the most intriguing variety of lightbulbs one could imagine. Everything on that desk broadcasted the occupant's job description as a senior lighting engineer with efficiency and panache.

Was this necessary? One could argue the lightbulbs were a symbol for others of what the occupant did, but they also were for him. They helped to create identity and a positive display of territoriality [31].

A tall, pink, signpost rises from this experience:

> **10) Moving at slow speed allows us to interact with people, but we still need symbols in the workplace for others and for our personal identity.**

Nestled in lightbulbs was a particularly intriguing filament globe that I couldn't take my eyes off and which blew my cover as a detached and unobtrusive observer. The occupant was quick to offer details about it with great passion, but his enthusiasm was replaced by mild resentment when he realised I was part of the design firm working on their new offices. "Are you taking away our desks?" he asked.

Although I didn't have the heart to reveal it at the time, the answer was yes. Our data indicated the average employee did not spend enough time at their desks to each warrant precious dedicated real estate. We proposed "a change to the environment that would increase choice", which is code for: "yes, you will lose your desk." Ten years have passed, and while I have forgotten all the technicalities of that lightbulb, I have not forgotten the lighting engineer and his passion.

That passionate engineer is now likely without lightbulbs or his own desk.

At the time of our observations and with the understanding we had, the solution made perfect sense, but that is only if the purpose of office buildings is to fill them up with as many employees as possible. This is not meant to be a cynical remark, it's not hard to formulate the wrong view if one is too close to the project and too immersed in the doing. Designers' days are peppered with meetings with stakeholders who focus on square metres per person and dollars, and this takes us to an important signpost:

11) The process of designing a workplace can get in the way of creating an environment which meets its purpose.

The key to this signpost is not to confuse practicalities such as budget and space constraints with the real purpose of the workplace.

Back on my pilgrimage, I left the petrol station and bid goodbye to its eccentric owner. As the door closed behind me, I got another warning: "camp on this side of the bridge, there are idiots on the other side." The warnings about the idiots were piling up.

Open Access This chapter is licensed under the terms of the Creative Commons Attribution 4.0 International License (http://creativecommons.org/licenses/by/4.0/), which permits use, sharing, adaptation, distribution and reproduction in any medium or format, as long as you give appropriate credit to the original author(s) and the source, provide a link to the Creative Commons license and indicate if changes were made.

The images or other third party material in this chapter are included in the chapter's Creative Commons license, unless indicated otherwise in a credit line to the material. If material is not included in the chapter's Creative Commons license and your intended use is not permitted by statutory regulation or exceeds the permitted use, you will need to obtain permission directly from the copyright holder.

Chapter 14
My Backpack

My backpack was very sturdy and if I interpreted what Ballistic Nylon Fabric meant correctly, it was bullet proof too. I carried two packs: a big one with a 70 litre capacity and a small 15 litre one which I wore in front to balance the weight of the larger pack on my back. I'd originally purchased the packs for an overseas trek that required something sturdy to endure rocky terrain and the better-not-to-know things that happen when one checks in their luggage on an international flight.

However, the same features that made the packs ideal for previous treks made them a poor choice for this one. My bullet-proof bags were heavy.

Then, six days into the walk, the waist belt on the backpack started to flop around like an untucked shirt. The belt itself was not the issue, but I had lost quite a bit of fat around my waist with all the walking. I got some duct-tape and a thick strip of foam that I attached to the inside of the belt – instant fat, problem solved.

I continued to add foam as necessary to ensure a tight fit that enabled the weight of the pack to be distributed across my hip bones and not my shoulders. I also added strips that I cut from a high-visibility vest to the front and back of the backpacks and lastly, fitted bicycle lights for additional visibility during the pitch-black, pre-dawn walks, Fig. 14.1 gives you the idea.

Over time and distance, both packs evolved to become something fully customised, incredibly practical, and deeply unattractive. If I'd been presented with this final version at the shop, I would never have purchased them, but by the time I got to the end of my walk I liked the backpacks even more not only because of how they fit, but for the story they told.

Similarly, in the workplace we might strive for the aspirational beauty of the impersonal over the ugliness of the personal. The pictures of workplaces in glossy architectural magazines preserve aspirational beauty, perhaps to maintain a general appeal before employees have the opportunity to make them their own.

© The Author(s) 2022
A. Chevez, *The Pilgrim's Guide to the Workplace*, SpringerBriefs in Business,
https://doi.org/10.1007/978-981-19-4759-9_14

Fig. 14.1 My backpacks and their added contraptions

A signpost about making something yours:

> **12) There is beauty in the ugliness of personalisation.**

As I was customising and improving my packs, I also wondered how I could make them lighter. The combined weight of both was somewhere between 15 and 20 kg, depending on what food and water I carried and whether my tent was dry or not. Early on I estimated my towel weighed as much as a banana and I could eat a banana. So, goodbye towel.

I didn't belabour the decision; I rationalised I wasn't using my towel, after all I was walking alone. Along the same line, I figured once I got further North and reached warmer weather, I could post my heavy winter clothing home. But when the time came to lighten my load, I didn't post a single item. Instead, I tucked the warm clothes into the least accessible part of my pack and made the decision to carry the same weight with which I started – minus the towel.

Yes, it was unnecessary deadweight for several hundred kilometres, and I went through some phenomenally steep sections where I was reminded of the way gravity pulls down matter. I rationalised what some might say was a dumb decision to carry unnecessary weight as bringing me closer to Sisyphus and his boulder.

It seems absurd if you only focus on the extra effort required to carry dead weight. If instead we consider the task as purposeful, it may result in an experience that delivers greater meaning. Is it better to go with the optimal rational option, or the absurdly meaningful one?

My choice surprised me and pointed to another signpost:

> **13) Absurdity can result in greater meaning and purpose.**

Open Access This chapter is licensed under the terms of the Creative Commons Attribution 4.0 International License (http://creativecommons.org/licenses/by/4.0/), which permits use, sharing, adaptation, distribution and reproduction in any medium or format, as long as you give appropriate credit to the original author(s) and the source, provide a link to the Creative Commons license and indicate if changes were made.

The images or other third party material in this chapter are included in the chapter's Creative Commons license, unless indicated otherwise in a credit line to the material. If material is not included in the chapter's Creative Commons license and your intended use is not permitted by statutory regulation or exceeds the permitted use, you will need to obtain permission directly from the copyright holder.

Chapter 15
Award Winning Scones

Whenever I walked into a small country town I looked for 'award winning' signs. These were usually written on folding boards standing outside bakeries letting passers-by know they had the best pies, vanilla slices, or scones in town. I trusted these accreditations more than the TripAdvisor Certificate of Excellence stickers on shop windows.

At the end of one day's walk, I was lured into a teashop by an 'award winning scones' sign. And it was true, the scones were good, but the true winner was the home grown, homemade, blood-plum jam. Hoping I could have it again for breakfast I asked the elderly lady minding the shop about opening times. "Between 10 and 10:30am, depending how fast my dog walks" she said, pointing to a dog sprawled on the shop floor. Judging by the old dog's appearance, opening time would be closer to 11am.

I mentioned my planned 6am departure and she directed me to a two-tier stack of jars of blood-plum jam for sale. Clearly, I wasn't the first person to have complimented her jam. After debating if a jar of jam was a worthy contributor to my Sisyphus' boulder, I decided to pass up the opportunity.

She then said, "sometimes memories are just as good," and her expression took on a faraway look. She continued,

> when I was 10, I was in Alicante [Spain] with my Mum. We were sitting at a restaurant next to the beach and a group of young boys had gone spearfishing and caught some octopus for us. They came back past us and proudly showed them to Mum and me on their way to the kitchen. I was disgusted by the slimy things, but Mum told me I needed to be polite and eat it when it was served.

And just like that, the elderly lady snapped back to where we were and went silent. Intrigued by where this conversation was heading, I asked if she had enjoyed the octopus.

"I can't remember," she replied, going back behind the shop counter, "but I do remember Alicante because of the octopus."

I never quite understood what she was trying to tell me, but the conversation influenced my thoughts during the rest of my pilgrimage. As I walked, I entertained myself imagining employees' arrival times at the office determined by how fast their pet could walk. Smiling I chuckled at how the all-too-common bottle necks we see in the morning in the foyers of office buildings in the city could be solve in this low-tech way.

And the octopus? Forget coordinates on a map, just use food to pinpoint locations.

My thinking reminded me of the frog and elephant-like ideas I had entertained 2 years earlier during my sleepless night after that flight back from Sydney. I imagined if that elderly lady had *evolved* in her own Galapagos Island, she might have developed a time-space construct based on pets and food. In such a world, people would make plans to catch up at the corner of *plums and carrots* when Mary's *cat returns*. This led me to think about their notion of work and their workplaces, and the subsequent societies they would spawn.

The thoughts were absurd, silly, and unnecessary. But so too is standing in a packed lobby waiting for a lift in the morning because no one has bothered to question the logic of an ingrained habit.

These absurdities can be summarised in the following signposts:

> **14) Seeing normality through absurdity can show the absurd as normal.**

> **15) Normality can be the offspring of the unchallenged.**

I am sure we can all think of something silly, even unnecessary, at our workplace which has been normalised simply because it remains unquestioned. Examples others have shared include questioning why we need to go to the same place over and over to work from 9 to 5.

Undoubtedly, there were many negatives of COVID-19, but one positive was that it not only challenged the status quo, but also proved we could do things differently and effectively.

Open Access This chapter is licensed under the terms of the Creative Commons Attribution 4.0 International License (http://creativecommons.org/licenses/by/4.0/), which permits use, sharing, adaptation, distribution and reproduction in any medium or format, as long as you give appropriate credit to the original author(s) and the source, provide a link to the Creative Commons license and indicate if changes were made.

The images or other third party material in this chapter are included in the chapter's Creative Commons license, unless indicated otherwise in a credit line to the material. If material is not included in the chapter's Creative Commons license and your intended use is not permitted by statutory regulation or exceeds the permitted use, you will need to obtain permission directly from the copyright holder.

Chapter 16
The Good, the Bad, and the Ugly

As the towns along the way got smaller the 'award-winning' signs and their competition began to disappear. One small town had nothing more than a pub that doubled as a post office – a default winner for my patronage. However, the experience of this small-town pub was in sharp contrast to the scones and jam of larger towns.

Entering pubs in a small town felt like stepping into a spaghetti western movie. You have seen it before, there is the outsider (me) approaching a buzzing bar through a pair of swinging saloon doors, the patrons cease their chatter and lift their eyes from their hands of poker (or phones) and fix their silent gaze on the stranger coming through the doors with an almost practiced precision.

Sure, my get-up, Fig. 16.1, and possibly the result of not having a towel and not showering as frequently as I should have may have contributed to the unsolicited attention. But I think it was the close-knit quality of small towns, where everyone knows everyone else, that made me stand out.

Off the main tourist routes, the strong social cohesion in small country towns was palpable. I could see how people talked to others at nearby tables as if the table itself was being stretched by an invisible social bond that drew them together.

I sat alone and listened to Morricone's iconic *The good, the bad and the ugly* [32] soundtrack playing in my mind and began to think about the good, bad and ugly sides of small-town dynamics. What is good about small towns is the way communities rally around those in need. In larger towns and cities it is easier to walk past, ignoring the misfortunes of those we don't know.

The bad side is what I experienced, the us and them alienation. I attributed the patrons' reactions to the common dislike of the unfamiliar and would like to believe that if I stayed longer that I too might be chatting across tables. If I went to the pub in my full gear every time, perhaps I might be accepted and deemed the 'town eccentric'.

© The Author(s) 2022
A. Chevez, *The Pilgrim's Guide to the Workplace*, SpringerBriefs in Business, https://doi.org/10.1007/978-981-19-4759-9_16

Fig. 16.1 My Sunday-best pub attire

The ugly side is when ongoing coexistence leads to the further alienation of outsiders, or those who are not part of the small-town social bond, labelling them forever as an unwelcomed stranger. You are probably already one step ahead of me on the similarities of this and what many experience in workplaces.

Like many things, this is like a double-edged sword. A highly cohesive team reaps similar benefits of a small town, potentially leading to increased performance. But the same team might also suffer from stale ideas or lack the performance that comes from the input of new players who challenge the status quo. This challenge to both, teams and organisations, is highlighted in the next signpost:

16) Strong cohesion can have the benefits and pitfalls of a small country town.

As a workplace researcher I am a strong advocate for the use of Social Network Analysis (SNA), the offspring of an unlikely collaboration between mathematicians, anthropologists, and sociologists that allows us to visualise and explore the threads of the social fabric holding together an organisation [33].

To properly define SNA is necessary to introduce more terms in need of further definitions. To avoid such a lengthy explanation, I will explain SNA by way of an example. In a small organisation, or a country town, a SNA would validate the already known social structure understood by most good publicans. Who interacts with who, and who doesn't. But as the organisation grows, SNA can also reveal surprises, including biases about peoples' interactions. Since biases are part of the organisational culture, some organisations can be blind to them.

To illustrate, SNA revealed a marked gender bias in one organisation we studied. Women were under-represented in exchanging ideas below what would have been expected from the demographic split. We discovered the organisation's employees were more inclined to discuss ideas with men than with women. Including the women.

In this situation, making the environment more social through the addition of places to connect and talk might not be the solution. As it turned out, women were over-represented in social interactions, but were still excluded from some idea-exchanging conversations. This in itself is an interesting signpost, suggesting increased socialisation does not guarantee involvement in organisational-shaping activities:

17) Increasing opportunities to socialise might not result in a more inclusive environment.

The need to understand the social fabric of organisations and the role that the environment plays in shaping it, is increasing as the nature of work (whatever we will end up doing) becomes more human, ergo more social.

Open Access This chapter is licensed under the terms of the Creative Commons Attribution 4.0 International License (http://creativecommons.org/licenses/by/4.0/), which permits use, sharing, adaptation, distribution and reproduction in any medium or format, as long as you give appropriate credit to the original author(s) and the source, provide a link to the Creative Commons license and indicate if changes were made.

The images or other third party material in this chapter are included in the chapter's Creative Commons license, unless indicated otherwise in a credit line to the material. If material is not included in the chapter's Creative Commons license and your intended use is not permitted by statutory regulation or exceeds the permitted use, you will need to obtain permission directly from the copyright holder.

Chapter 17
Rubbish Snakes

Choosing to walk in cold temperatures to avoid encounters with some of the world's most venomous snakes paid off. I only saw one of them on the entire walk and we seemed equally frightened of each other. I am sure that if snakes could scream, it would have yelled as loudly as I did.

Sad for the environment but luckily for me, I saw plenty more of snake-like rubbish in the form of sinuous belts, cables, or other rubbish than real snakes, Fig. 17.1. The rural roads were mostly clean, but I quickly discovered how I could tell when I was approaching a town: the amount of litter ballooned. To pass time I imagined the smoking habits of the local population from the discarded cigarette packets or their aversion to sleep by the number of half-crushed cans of energy drinks.

Those cans reminded me of 'z-sups'. Similar to energy drinks, these are sleep suppressing pills depicted in the comic *Power Nap* [34] that allow people to work up to 20 hours a day doing meaningless things. Ironically people in the comic work such long hours so that they are able to afford the pills – the circle of life. The main character is allergic to z-sups and needs to sleep, which is seen as a disability.

Back to my roadside analyses, I imagine the local population growth based on the results of pregnancy testing kits strewn along the verges – most were negative. If gender reveal parties had been a fad back then, I would also have been able to further my demographic study by analysing the colour of discarded confetti.

But when it comes to leftovers in the workplace, what can we potentially learn? A lot. Not so much from looking at the contents of rubbish bins, but by looking at the digital by-product of operations in organisations, a concept which Wharton professor Christian Terwiesch refers to as 'digital exhaust' [35]. Big tech companies like Microsoft are investing heavily into this way of understanding organisations.

I had the opportunity to co-design a research project [36] where we measured a more analogous type of leftover: noise, as a by-product of face-to-face interactions. The idea was to overlap noise measurements with social network data to discover a way to use noise as a proxy for knowledge transfer in open plan settings. We called our project *The Sound of Collaboration*.

Fig. 17.1 'Rubbish snake' collection

One of the acoustic engineers involved in the research explained the difference between a noise and a sound in a way which is hard to forget: "a noise is an unpleasant sound." Perhaps we could turn noise in the workplace into sound if we are able to assign it a value of knowledge transfer.

17 Rubbish Snakes

Of course, information travels within an organisation silently through emails, but as already emphasised by others [37], the interactions that underpin collaboration, as opposed to a mere exchange of information, benefit from gestures and non-verbal communication. These synchronous, unstructured interactions are better supported by face-to-face interactions, which are often noisy. Hence the following signpost:

> **18) The noise of knowledge transfer could be the sound of collaboration.**

Open Access This chapter is licensed under the terms of the Creative Commons Attribution 4.0 International License (http://creativecommons.org/licenses/by/4.0/), which permits use, sharing, adaptation, distribution and reproduction in any medium or format, as long as you give appropriate credit to the original author(s) and the source, provide a link to the Creative Commons license and indicate if changes were made.

The images or other third party material in this chapter are included in the chapter's Creative Commons license, unless indicated otherwise in a credit line to the material. If material is not included in the chapter's Creative Commons license and your intended use is not permitted by statutory regulation or exceeds the permitted use, you will need to obtain permission directly from the copyright holder.

Chapter 18
Where Are the Idiots?

The warnings about the idiots concerned me. 'The idiots' were presumably so not because of their dim intelligence, but because they were out there to cause trouble. Most concerning of all was the way in which the people voicing these warnings looked at me. They tilted their head ever so slightly, distorted their mouth as if tasting a lemon, and squinted their eyes – I didn't stand a chance against the idiots.

Thankfully, I didn't cross paths with a single idiot. Instead, I came across people who were only too happy to extend kind gestures like serving me conspicuously extra-large portions of food along with a big smile and a cheerful "this will get you going!".

On one occasion as I was preparing to pay for an iced coffee at a roadside petrol station, the attendant offered nutritional advice, "those are full of sugar; they are not good for you. I will make you a real coffee!" Minutes later she returned with my 'real coffee' plus a packet of biscuits. What was that about the sugar?

It was too early for the service station to be busy, and we both had time for coffee and a chat. She said she had thought about leaving everything behind and go for a long walk herself, but she offered no clues as to where she wanted to go. I supposed it didn't matter as long as it was away from the shop, her husband, and her kids – although she quickly clarified she loved them, but at times just wanted to get away from it all. I chose to keep my comments to myself and offer a sympathetic ear only. Though I knew it takes more than a chat with a stranger to kick-start a pilgrimage, I feared providing too much encouragement could result in a kid waking up crying after a vanished parent.

Other wishful pilgrims emerged along the journey in the shape of a baker, a gardener, and others whose professions I couldn't tell. These were all strangers opening up to me and sharing their dreams in life in ways I haven't experienced before, or after, the walk.

I wondered what prompted all these people to speak so honestly and freely about personal matters, and eventually concluded it was my appearance. I had the look of a walker and that evoked romanticised ideas of following one's dreams as well as an invitation to share their own dreams. Had I been an undercover pilgrim, walking in ordinary street clothes, my interactions might have been as impersonal and humdrum as they usually are.

Similarly, how a workplace looks is important, but not so much in its pursuit of style – we have to be careful not to fall into the trap of confusing good taste for good design [38]. How a workplace looks is important because it communicates the ambitions of the people and organisation it houses. The looks of a workplace can influence the interactions an organisation has with its employees and clients. Looks are important and they go beyond beauty.

So, if the idea of following one's dreams looks like a pair of boots, walking sticks, a backpack, and a big hat, what should the idea of 'work' look like?

This question gains further relevance when considered from a wider perspective of what design is. In a Harvard Business Review article, Tim Brown, the CEO of IDEO, wrote:

> *Historically, design has been treated as a downstream step in the development process – the point where designers, who have played no earlier role in the substantive work of innovation, come along and put a beautiful wrapper around the idea.* [39]

Brown then lures us to consider "*dramatic new forms of value*" if designers were to create the idea itself. Imagine what might arise if workplace designers were involved in designing the idea of work first, and then its wrapper. Hence the two signposts below:

19) Designing work first and then the workplace could lead to dramatic new forms of value.

20) Good design aligns the work aesthetic of an organisation with its looks.

A good design would then be that which wraps up an organisation with its inherently unique look of work. The resemblance of workplaces, even those of organisations in different sectors, suggests this view is not widely shared. However, an authenticity of appearance might allow organisation to encounter more dreamers and avoid the idiots.

Open Access This chapter is licensed under the terms of the Creative Commons Attribution 4.0 International License (http://creativecommons.org/licenses/by/4.0/), which permits use, sharing, adaptation, distribution and reproduction in any medium or format, as long as you give appropriate credit to the original author(s) and the source, provide a link to the Creative Commons license and indicate if changes were made.

The images or other third party material in this chapter are included in the chapter's Creative Commons license, unless indicated otherwise in a credit line to the material. If material is not included in the chapter's Creative Commons license and your intended use is not permitted by statutory regulation or exceeds the permitted use, you will need to obtain permission directly from the copyright holder.

Chapter 19
Winds

I experienced my fair share of days walking in severe, gusty wind. The weather alert on my phone warned me of peak gusts of over 90 km/h and when it did, I relied on my walking sticks to keep me upright. I also paid extra attention to potential falling branches and even entire trees – gum trees have notoriously shallow roots. Strong wind also made for noticeably longer, or shorter, walking days depending on the wind's direction and it played a role in whether camping was hard or simply impossible.

On one of these days the pegs that secure my tent to the Earth refused to stay in the ground, causing the tent to behave more like a kite than a shelter. While wrestling to set up my home for the night I spotted a bare patch of land next to a coffee shop on the opposite side of the road and decided it would be a better place to set-up as the building would shield me from the wind.

My plan met an abrupt end when the shop manager came out.

He told me the shop's owner had a strict no camping policy. He was nice about it; he had seen my many failed attempts to keep my tent on the ground. Once he realised that I was travelling on foot and had limited options in where I could spend the night, he phoned the owner hoping to overturn the 'no camping next to the coffeeshop' rule.

A harsh 'no' spilled over the phone in the tone of someone annoyed at being disturbed by such a trivial thing. Unable to convey the significance of iguanas in the Galapagos Island in workplace design over the phone, the café manager tried one last time before the owner hung up without a goodbye. Genuinely sorry, the manager looked at me and tilted his head, as if to say, "well, I tried."

The café was in the middle of nowhere and it was getting dark. I was tired. The wind refused to let me set up my tent and the rain was about to start. If ever there was a time for violins to play in the background, this was it.

As I was packing my gear a voice broke through my intense concentration, which was not for packing, but for thinking about where I was going to spend the night.

"Oi" the voice said, "I'm the cook. I'll finish my shift soon and can drive you into town."

Clearly word had spread. I jumped at the offer knowing it involved a detour into town that would add several kilometres to my next day's walk. That night I slept under a roof with four walls firmly attached to the ground. It still rained, but I was safe and dry inside my room.

The next morning, I used the extra steps from the detour to think about empathy. In particular, how empathy seems to become stronger the closer we are to the situation. A sort of a radius of empathy, in which its effects decay as the radius increases.

I can only speculate that the owner of the café might have shown empathy if he had been there and seen me struggle with my tent. He might not have let me camp there, for a variety of good reasons, but he might have been more sympathetic about it – maybe even suggested an alternative, like his staff did.

A signpost with a compelling reason for having people collocated at the workplace:

21) Social proximity can promote empathy.

Fortunately, not every day was windy. Some were calm, sunny, crisp winter's days. One of those days was perfect.

Open Access This chapter is licensed under the terms of the Creative Commons Attribution 4.0 International License (http://creativecommons.org/licenses/by/4.0/), which permits use, sharing, adaptation, distribution and reproduction in any medium or format, as long as you give appropriate credit to the original author(s) and the source, provide a link to the Creative Commons license and indicate if changes were made.

The images or other third party material in this chapter are included in the chapter's Creative Commons license, unless indicated otherwise in a credit line to the material. If material is not included in the chapter's Creative Commons license and your intended use is not permitted by statutory regulation or exceeds the permitted use, you will need to obtain permission directly from the copyright holder.

Chapter 20
The Perfect Day

Day 30 was a short 13 km walk from Mollymook Beach to Conjola in NSW. It was one of the shortest walks of the whole pilgrimage and I covered it in less than 3 hours. Weatherwise, I wished I had spent more time on the road on that sunny day which was pleasantly cool and completely devoid of my nemesis wind.

I had enjoyed a sound night's sleep and there was literally a real spring in my step, my pack was at its lightest because my tent was dry and I knew I could get away with only 1 l (1 kg) of water for such a short walk. My mood was so favourable that I decided to ditch my boring standard breakfast of granola bars, salted peanuts, and a banana washed down with one of those big full of sugar iced coffees. Instead, I had a real coffee and a cooked breakfast at Milton, a quaint place with beautiful heritage buildings.

As I finished my bacon and eggs with a side order of avocado, I realised that I was *only* some 200 km away from Sydney. Rejoicing, I settled back in my seat, ordered scones, a second coffee and began to mentally recap my trip. The optimism of the day led me to reflect on the pilgrimage with a mindset of having already completed it. I anticipated the stories I would tell and write, including those that didn't fit in these chapters.

Intriguingly, my thoughts went back to the adversities I faced up to that day. I remembered how stiff and sore my whole body was after walking the length of a marathon (just over 42 km) across an undulating terrain and knowing I would not be greeted by a cheering crowd and a sports drink. I also thought about the day I wore every single item of clothing I carried to try to keep warm, but still shivered with cold and wondered why my trusty sleeping bag that kept me toasty warm on a previous trek to the top of Mount Kilimanjaro barely kept out the chill of the night. And then, there was the blood that I had found coming out of my left ear just 2 days ago. I would have to wait a few days to reach a clinic and find out what was going on.

The troubles with my ear turned out to be an infection from the earplugs I wore to buffer the noise, definitely not sound, of the traffic. My rationale was that if I wasn't talking to anyone or receiving input from the outside world through my ears, why take the earplugs off? It was a great idea, until it wasn't, and an infection set in. I then swapped the plugs for earmuffs, Fig. 20.1.

But on that day, none of this mattered – it was as I said, a perfect day. Contemplating these personal war stories led me to conclude that in just 29 days I had been challenged in so many ways and had faced daily uncertainty about things I took for granted like having water, food, and a warm and dry place to sleep.

But most challenging of all, far beyond the soreness, cold, isolation, winds, hunger, thirst, tiredness, boredom, troubled ear, mythical idiots, and everything else that the road threw at me, were the bloody double-trailer trucks. These were incredibly big trucks that made me feel foolish for not thinking about them while planning my walk.

The risks of snakes and bushfires fit with my romanticised idea of a pilgrimage. I saw myself walking through grass fields surrounded by idyllic nature and am pretty confident that the dreamers I crossed paths with also pictured themselves in a similar way. Never did huge trucks travelling at impossibly fast speeds come into my image of a pilgrimage.

Unless it was safer to walk in the same direction as the traffic, which was the case if there was only one shoulder available, I would walk against the oncoming traffic. Naively, I hoped I would be agile enough to dodge a speeding oncoming truck while carrying two backpacks. I stuck with this nerve-wracking practice of seeing constant traffic heading towards me, even after a few close calls when all I could do was to close my eyes.

Particularly stressful were the sections of road where the shoulder was too narrow, or there was no shoulder at all.

Fig. 20.1 Earmuffs

20 The Perfect Day

As if pilgrimages had a pre-set quota of discomfort, vicissitudes, and life-threatening situations, that I had now already endured, I decided on that perfect day that all troubles were behind me. Rejoicing and encouraged by that thought, I finished my coffee, put on my two backpacks, and hit the road.

Everything remained perfect as I reached the outskirts of Milton. But eventually the perfect footpath turned into just a shoulder on the road and then, as it had done so many times before, the shoulder disappeared. I kept the spring in my step until the chilling turbulence of a truck's side-draft hit me.

This didn't bother me much, though I would usually end up with dirt which somehow found its way into my mouth, and I was left chewing on sand (I chose to think it was sand) for the next few hundred metres. However, after one too many close calls, I came to dread this 'road spray' by association.

Another truck flew past me.

I don't know how close it was, that didn't matter. I felt betrayed. After everything I'd gone through, I shouldn't be going through this anymore! My heart was pounding as if I was sprinting up a hill, and yet I hadn't moved an inch – I couldn't. I was in the throes of a panic attack that pinned me to the spot where the truck had sprayed me.

I was too scared to move. The notion of 'only 200 km to go', arguably a bit less by now, seemed an impossible feat to accomplish. Slowly, I unclipped the backpacks from each other and let them slip from my shoulders. Hearing the packs hit the road brought an instant relief.

It was over.

The moment allowed me to regain my thoughts which were rushing ahead with an urgency that made my mind spin. I struggled to simultaneously make sense of the situation I found myself in and come up with a plan to get back home.

> "So, is this where it ends?" I asked myself, "I should probably move my packs because they are too close to the traffic. Should I hitchhike back to Milton? Should I rename my pilgrimage 'Sisyphus goes to Milton'?"

It was in the depth of those thoughts, standing next to a busy road north of Milton with the now impossible 200 km to go, that the absurdity of my situation hit me.

Here I was, a middle-aged Mexican in the middle of nowhere, all alone, walking to Sydney. I had no towel or charity, and I was finding meaning in discarded rubbish and pink aeroplanes. I was at risk of getting flattened by a truck and there was dirt, I mean sand, in my mouth. All of this because 2 years earlier I read about the iguanas in the Galapagos Islands on a commuter flight and somehow, they led me to believe it was a good idea to put my life on hold to walk a ridiculous distance, carrying unnecessary clothes, without music, but with an ear infection. All of this in hope of incubating a unique idea about how to design better workplaces!

The absurdity of the situation floored me.

And when I was at rock-bottom, I became empowered by the thought that no machine could ever come up with such nonsense that contained so much purpose and meaning. I felt incredibly human, and my very human panic and distress subsided. I yanked both backpacks back over my shoulders, clipped them tight and began walking again.

This is where Signpost 2 emerged, and if Signpost 13 hadn't already highlighted the role of absurdity in the creation of purpose, then it would have risen here too.

The distance to Sydney was no longer 'just' or 'impossible' 200 km away; the distance didn't matter anymore. I knew I was going to get there.

In a way, my pilgrimage started then and there – it really was the perfect day.

Open Access This chapter is licensed under the terms of the Creative Commons Attribution 4.0 International License (http://creativecommons.org/licenses/by/4.0/), which permits use, sharing, adaptation, distribution and reproduction in any medium or format, as long as you give appropriate credit to the original author(s) and the source, provide a link to the Creative Commons license and indicate if changes were made.

The images or other third party material in this chapter are included in the chapter's Creative Commons license, unless indicated otherwise in a credit line to the material. If material is not included in the chapter's Creative Commons license and your intended use is not permitted by statutory regulation or exceeds the permitted use, you will need to obtain permission directly from the copyright holder.

Chapter 21
The Very Last Step

Flying to Sydney for work came with the promise of exciting conversations and felt as though I fitted a week's worth of work into a single day. In contrast, my Sisyphus goes to Sydney arrival had no meetings or conferences scheduled, nor any coffee catchups to go to. There was only one thing I had to do once I arrived in Sydney and that was to get a flight back home to Melbourne.

I wondered how it would feel to arrive in Sydney under one's own steam from the day I began planning the pilgrimage. Would I fall on my knees, raise my arms, and turn my teary face towards the sky, or do a Forrest Gump and laconically declare, "*I'm pretty tired, I think I'll go home now*" [40]. I wouldn't have to wait much longer to find out. I was on my last walking day, only 37 km away from the Sydney Opera House, my pilgrimage finishing line.

Eight hours from the finish might seem like a long walk, but from the perspective of life at 4.6 km/h it actually felt shorter than the minutes spent waiting in a line to board a flight. My modest contribution to *Learning from Las Vegas* notion of speed of travel would be that in addition to symbols, our patience is also affected, but in a proportionally inverse way: increased speed results in decreased patience. At the cruising speed of jet planes (~200 times walking speed) our patience is tiny.

As I got closer to the Opera House, the long-forgotten imaginary travelling companion I'd met on day one appeared from nowhere. Once again, I was strangely compelled to follow his fast pace. On reflection, the pilgrimage was like a hard-to-chew crusty old bread sandwich with a delicious filling. The best part was the in-between, the days in the centre of my walk, but they still needed a top and bottom to hold it all together.

Finally, I took step 1,281,772 at the base of the Sydney Opera House. I was paying so much attention to how I was feeling and even how I should feel, that I am not sure how I truly felt.

What I can say is that every thought was overwhelmed by the surreal experience of finally being there. That surreal moment when the *there* becomes the here. I was surprised by how significant and special it felt, even though I had stood in this place many times before. Now of course, it was how I had reached the Opera House which made it feel, and look, so different.

A lot of what we do in workplace design has to do with this formula:

$$B = f(P, E)$$

In which:

B is behaviour, *P* is person and *E* is the environment.

It reads as behaviour is a function of the person and their environment and it's the brainchild of psychologist Kurt Lewin [41]. It's an elegant formula, but it's also a conceptual one and cannot be used in the same way as mathematical formulae. That this is sometimes overlooked is the source of many misunderstandings in workplace design.

Designers focus their attention on the (E)nvironment side of the equation and their aim is to shape it in a way that will promote certain (B)ehaviour. Robert Bechtel's words fit well here: *"behaviour, not space, is enclosed by architecture"* [42]. The (P)erson is also considered and personas are created. However, once conceived, these personas are for all intents and purposes thought to be constant – closer to demographic stereotypes, than humans.

This logic felt incredibly flawed on the steps of the Opera House, where I sat, rediscovering it as if I was looking at it for the first time.

Granted, we don't usually go through experiences as intense as my pilgrimage on a daily basis in the workplace. However, according to Lewin, physically identical environments can feel different under much less dramatic circumstances, for instance when a person is hungry and when the person is satiated.

It then begs the question, what matters most, the qualities of the environment, or the state of the person? On this, Lewin provides the type of academic answer which frustrates many:

> *...depends upon the state of the person and at the same time on the environment, although their relative importance is different in different cases.* [41]

Some scholars [43] have also commented that the comma between 'P' and 'E' in the formula (rather than a plus or minus sign, or any other operator) leaves their relationship open. Regardless of this, Lewin's formula is a useful reminder and an important signpost for those working with the (E)nvironment, not to forget about the changing nature of the (P)erson.

> **22) (B)ehaviour in the workplace can vary as a result of changes in the (E)nvironment and/or the (P)erson.**

While still meandering around the Opera House, I also thought about how unremarkable that one last step felt. It truly was remarkably similar to the step before

21 The Very Last Step

Fig. 21.1 Selfies at Federation Square, Melbourne, 1 July 2018 (top) –Sydney Opera House, 11 August 2018 (bottom)

that one, and pretty similar to the one before that. However, in between the first and the last step there were over a million and two hundred thousand of tiny and unnoticeable changes where the pilgrimage happened. Cue the song *From little things, big things grow* [44], but I didn't feel any bigger, just different. The selfies, Fig. 21.1, offer a hint of some subtle physical changes, unruly hair and beard. But the photos fail to capture that it is a different (P)erson.

After a long, long shower at a hotel and sleeping off the tiredness of 42 days, I took a flight back to Melbourne.

Open Access This chapter is licensed under the terms of the Creative Commons Attribution 4.0 International License (http://creativecommons.org/licenses/by/4.0/), which permits use, sharing, adaptation, distribution and reproduction in any medium or format, as long as you give appropriate credit to the original author(s) and the source, provide a link to the Creative Commons license and indicate if changes were made.

The images or other third party material in this chapter are included in the chapter's Creative Commons license, unless indicated otherwise in a credit line to the material. If material is not included in the chapter's Creative Commons license and your intended use is not permitted by statutory regulation or exceeds the permitted use, you will need to obtain permission directly from the copyright holder.

Chapter 22
Mind Lag

12 August 2018. 3pm.
30,000 ft above New South Wales.

I looked through the aeroplane window and I couldn't believe my eyes when I recognised the route I had taken on my approach to Sydney. I grabbed my phone and took a picture of a distinctive section of the road that I had covered on day 32 of the walk, from Sanctuary Point (covered by the wing on the right) to Bomaderry (under the low-level clouds on the left) indicated with an 'x', Fig. 22.1.

In the middle of the upper photo, marked with a square, is the bridge crossing the Shoalhaven River that I photographed while walking, lower picture.

I covered 34 km on that day and was on the road for 7 h and 40 min, remarkably close to my standard 7.5 h of work per day. But looking down from my window, that full day of work as a pilgrim disappeared from my field of view in a matter of seconds – it felt as surreal as the moment I arrived at the Sydney Opera House.

The plane then veered inland, and I lost sight of my pilgrimage route.

Sydney and Melbourne are connected by a flight of just over one hour and they are both in the Australian Eastern Standard Time zone. It would be inexplicable to experience any sort of jetlag on such a short hop, but I did experience an acute case of 'mind-lag' when I got home

Astoundingly, nothing relevant came up when I googled 'mind-lag' so I will offer my very own definition of the term.

> **Mind-lag** /mʌɪnd lag/ *noun*. The feeling experienced when the body seems to arrive before the mind.

A symptom of jet-lag is the struggle to stay awake or to fall asleep when one should be awake or asleep. In contrast, the symptoms of *mind-lag* include a spinning sensation in the head and repeatedly saying, either out loud or in one's mind: "I can't believe I am here!"

After re-uniting with my dusty backpack at the conveyor belt in the baggage reclaim area, I ditched my plans to take public transport home. Instead, I chose a

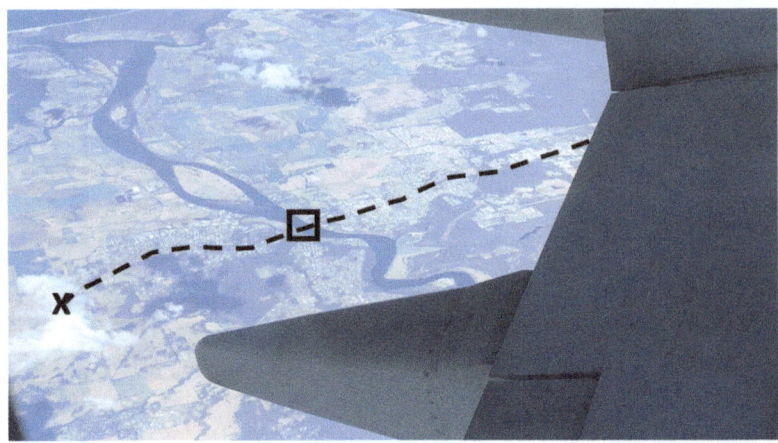

Fig. 22.1 Aeroplane view (top) and pilgrim's view (bottom)

scenic walk in hope my mind would catch up to where my body now found itself. A sort of self-medicating mind-lag treatment.

When I eventually reached my front door, I received the enlightenment that hadn't arrived when I had taken my last step at the Opera House: pilgrimages don't finish with the walk.

Open Access This chapter is licensed under the terms of the Creative Commons Attribution 4.0 International License (http://creativecommons.org/licenses/by/4.0/), which permits use, sharing, adaptation, distribution and reproduction in any medium or format, as long as you give appropriate credit to the original author(s) and the source, provide a link to the Creative Commons license and indicate if changes were made.

The images or other third party material in this chapter are included in the chapter's Creative Commons license, unless indicated otherwise in a credit line to the material. If material is not included in the chapter's Creative Commons license and your intended use is not permitted by statutory regulation or exceeds the permitted use, you will need to obtain permission directly from the copyright holder.

Part IV
Real Steps, Virtual Pilgrimage

Chapter 23
Virtual Pilgrimage, Real Pain

"What's next?" asked my friends and family after I returned. Their faces once showed confusion when I first told them about the iguanas and all of that, but now, they couldn't wait to hear what even crazier new adventure I had in store.

"I don't know", I replied. It was a small white lie because my plan was to regain the 10 kg I had lost from the walk and figure out what I had learnt from the pilgrimage. Sharing that would have deflated their excitement.

Returning to my day job, I felt an increased unease hovering around the edges of my approach to work. I felt that there were other, arguably more useful ways, to approach the way we design, deliver and measure what we consider to be a good place to work.

I suspected that keeping track of how many people use or don't use an office, or how satisfied employees are with their facilities, or the amount of energy the building consumes, and the many other things we typically measure were all necessary, but insufficient to satisfy even the dimmest version of what the Signposts point us toward.

In search of new metrics, I found a *Workplace Dignity Scale* [45] and in collaboration with a multi-disciplinary team of design practitioners and academics set out to explore if workplace design could help employees maintain and gain dignity.

We published our preliminary findings in a short report entitled *Designing for Dignity* [46]. A point worth mentioning here is that dignity is affirmed when people are treated as inherently worthy of respect, and that can be crystallised passively, yet pervasively, in the place they work.

Our *Designing for Dignity* study was essentially an exploratory way of looking at the workplace. It has a long way to go to earn its place alongside established methods. But even if it never gets there, it still serves as a reminder of what counts in the workplace. As the sociologist William B. Cameron wrote: *"Not everything that can be counted counts, and not everything that counts can be counted"* [47].

This presents an often-overlooked signpost:

> **23) The workplace is not only what we can measure.**

Slowly, my iguana – the promised epiphanies from my pilgrimage – started to take shape. On that front the going was slow, but I was making great progress on my other project. The kilos were piling a lot faster than the lessons. Eating chicken parmigiana with a sense of duty makes it taste even better.

Type Two Clarity

Many words have been written by people sharing their experiences of a pilgrimage's end. There are those who elaborate on the prevailing sense of emptiness post-walk, others grapple with the loss of purpose mixed with the loss of new, but intense, friendships made along the way.

Those who found the experience positive, but the aftermath complicated, seem to yearn for the simple days of just walking. Then there are those who were disappointed that the answers they set out to find just didn't come, at least not as fast as they had hoped for.

Maybe, just as there is Type Two Fun, there is also a Type Two Clarity? A clarity gained through time.

And then, 2020 came around.

Little did I know that my pilgrimage would resume two years after I walked to Sydney. This time it wasn't prompted by iguanas, nor by any other animal, but by our lives becoming increasingly more digital in response to the developing COVID-19 pandemic.

"Can a pilgrimage be done virtually?", I wondered.

It was a question I was glad I never had to think about, but an advertisement promoting an online version of El Camino de Santiago led me to ponder it. I clicked on the comments section beneath the post expecting to find an overwhelming consensus that the only way to do El Camino was at El Camino, in Spain – not via a website. It was quite the opposite and an overwhelming number of comments appeared in support:

Cool!
　I love this!
　I just finished The Camino [online] *and am thinking about doing The Inca trail* [online] *next.*

23 Virtual Pilgrimage, Real Pain

I kept scrolling. Surely, I'd find some comments from people who 'really knew' what they were talking about. Eventually, a long way down, I found one:

> *Fascinating how a path to 'god' or 'oneness' or at least the human quest for meaning, gets boiled down to something so trivial.*

The trivial part referred to how one does El Camino online: you walk anywhere you find yourself to be in the real world and upload the distance walked onto a website where an icon of yourself moves along the French route connecting the French Pyrenees to Santiago De Compostela in Spain.

Simple, and trivial.

Normally, I'm not this cynical, but this 'pilgrimage' was irritating me. On reflection, I realised what was bothering me; this pilgrimage wasn't done the way a pilgrimage is meant to be done and consequently, it changed what a pilgrimage is, or ought to be. The virtual Camino challenged underpinning notions about pilgrimages.

With such a realisation, so too came that my iguana was doing a similar thing, not to pilgrimages, but to workplaces. Ultimately, my evolved idea challenges underlying notions of the workplace.

In one of those moments, which I knew I would come to regret later, it came to me that I owed it to my iguana to overcome the distaste created by something that challenged my beliefs. I needed to give the virtual Camino de Santiago a fair go.

To be clear, I'm not advocating the unrestrained adoption of ideas which we might have good reasons to avoid. Rather, my suggestion is to reconsider those which we discard for no other reason than that they question our beliefs. I would say that a way to differentiate between these two is to examine the extent of the visceral reaction one has to the idea.

Of course, equally wrong can be accepting an idea just because it fits comfortably with one's view of the world. I amazed myself by how well I had managed to illustrate both sides of my bias by discrediting opposing views to mine about pilgrimages while seeking out those that aligned with my own.

Surprisingly, the online version of El Camino came pre-loaded with a very important feature of pilgrimages that I raised in Part 1: pain. While not physical, it was one of the greatest pains to human nature which Walter Bagehot warned us about in the nineteenth century, the pain of a new idea.

> *[A new idea] makes you think that after all, your favourite notions may be wrong, your firmest beliefs ill-founded. [48]*

The first signpost of the virtual pilgrimage appeared even before I paid for my registration:

24) The difficulty in changing our beliefs can hinder the adoption of innovation.

Back when I wrote my PhD thesis, I argued that the future of the workplace would be influenced by the process through which we adopt innovation. It's a bit of an underwhelming statement. However, adoption of innovation is far from being a rational straight forward process. Personal, corporate, and even industry biases within wider social and cultural contexts moderate the adoption of innovation [49]. Importantly, these biases are not mere inconveniences, they are extremely useful in helping us understand who we are and the type of futures we aspire to.

My Camino was virtual, but the 774 km required to complete it were all too real. I found myself once again walking an unnecessary number of kilometres for another ridiculous reason. On the upside, this virtual experiment offered the opportunity to experience a challenging idea – an important and necessary step in reshaping the future of work and the workplace. It also created a fertile context to contrast analogue with virtual worlds in ways that are particularly useful to work environments.

Open Access This chapter is licensed under the terms of the Creative Commons Attribution 4.0 International License (http://creativecommons.org/licenses/by/4.0/), which permits use, sharing, adaptation, distribution and reproduction in any medium or format, as long as you give appropriate credit to the original author(s) and the source, provide a link to the Creative Commons license and indicate if changes were made.

The images or other third party material in this chapter are included in the chapter's Creative Commons license, unless indicated otherwise in a credit line to the material. If material is not included in the chapter's Creative Commons license and your intended use is not permitted by statutory regulation or exceeds the permitted use, you will need to obtain permission directly from the copyright holder.

Chapter 24
Deconstructing Pilgrimages

The online Camino started in the beautiful Saint-Jean-Pied-De-Port, right at the foot of the French Pyrenees. This time there was not a small get-together at the starting point and that was a good thing, because I wasn't there either. I started the walk many thousands of kilometres away.

Every day, I walked the streets around my home and uploaded distances to a website. The process stayed trivial until the very end, but it also served as a constant reminder of the 17,000 km gap between where I was taking steps and where the pilgrimage was meant to occur, Fig. 24.1.

A few days in, I received an email from the organisers with an 'activity conversion' list. It turns out that I could record time spent doing other (preapproved) non-walking activities in the real world, and then convert that effort into virtual kilometres taking me ever closer to Santiago de Compostela.

The list included an eclectic collection of seemingly un-pilgrim-like activities such as dancing and ping pong. My favourite conversion activity was housework. If I am honest, I was hoping I could reverse the conversion and exchange all of my 774 km for its equivalent of over 200 hours of housekeeping, and then be exempted from that much of it in the real world. Sadly, my partner didn't buy it.

While I didn't use any conversion, they lead to an interesting question: is walking a necessary requirement of a pilgrimage? If we can, as we mostly do, walk without it being a pilgrimage, could the converse also be true?

I could hardly recognise myself. Not so long ago, I had been enraged by an ad promoting a virtual version of El Camino, a couple of days into it I was taking potshots at the very nature of pilgrimages.

However, my heresy paid off in two ways. First, I now believe that it is in fact possible to do a pilgrimage without walking. This is encouraging news to those who have asked me how they too could benefit from a similar experience of a pilgrimage without the steps. More on this on Chap. 32.

Fig. 24.1 Gap between the walk and the pilgrimage

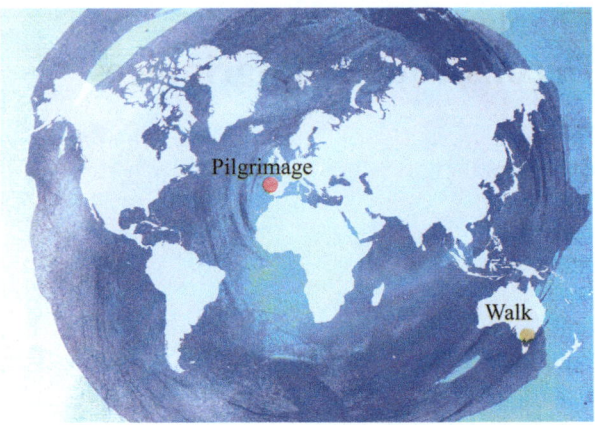

Second, the intangibility of a pilgrimage and the physicality of the walk seem strikingly similar to the intangibility of work and the tangibility of tasks. Decoupling a pilgrimage from its walk set me up for attempting a similar challenge with work and its tasks.

Two signposts emerged in quick succession:

25) Work and tasks are different yet interconnected.

26) Work is intangible, tasks are tangible.

Along this line of thought it became clear that both, pilgrimages and work, stand to lose a lot when we reduce them to their most common metrics: distance covered and its outputs. The ensuing signpost inevitably followed:

27) Work is more than its output.

I was on a roll and before I put my feet up for the day, another signpost came up:

28) The workplace could benefit from lessons derived from instances where work can't be done.

That last signpost came out of the realisation that our predominant view about work, and thereafter the workplace, comes from, wait for it... our ability to work. But are there lessons about work worth learning from instances in which work can't be done?

Imagine this:

It is 4:30am and you are awake and ready to go to work. You are starting the day early not because your commute is long, nor to finish early and sneak in a gym session before dinner. No, you are up that early to spend as much time as you can working.

If that sounds too keen or frankly unappealing, what if I also told you that you were not going to be paid for it? In fact, you will be trading objects for the privilege to work. Why? To have something to do.

This is not the plot of a post-Artificial Intelligence dystopian novel about a jobless society in which technology replaces humans. This was a case documented by researchers [50] almost three decades ago. This scenario happened in a prison where inmates would get up before dawn, exchange cigarettes and negotiate privileges to be able to do a job – for the sake of having something to do.

The job in question was to feed the fish in the fish tank.

Lessons from *"a state of preclusion from engagement in occupations of necessity and/or meaning due to factors that stand outside the immediate control of the individual"* [51], or *occupational deprivation environments* for short, would allow us to see work as more than a sum of its tasks. It could also help us design better places for when we do need to work.

Footprints in the Snow

In Agatha Christie's novel, *Murder on the Orient Express* [52] the motionless body of Mr. Ratchett is discovered with twelve stab wounds. As the mystery unfolds, we learn that a window of his train compartment was left open, suggesting the killer had escaped. But Hercule Poirot, the consummate detective, knew the killer was still on the train. There were no footprints in the snow outside.

While less dramatic than Christie's train setting, workplaces can also be approached as crime scenes where the environment provides clues into the nature of work done in them. Amongst the many clues, one that is the loudest and most common across workplaces is that it's all about productivity. But like in Mr. Ratchett's case, the most evident clue is also a misleading one. Like Poirot, we know better.

Open Access This chapter is licensed under the terms of the Creative Commons Attribution 4.0 International License (http://creativecommons.org/licenses/by/4.0/), which permits use, sharing, adaptation, distribution and reproduction in any medium or format, as long as you give appropriate credit to the original author(s) and the source, provide a link to the Creative Commons license and indicate if changes were made.

The images or other third party material in this chapter are included in the chapter's Creative Commons license, unless indicated otherwise in a credit line to the material. If material is not included in the chapter's Creative Commons license and your intended use is not permitted by statutory regulation or exceeds the permitted use, you will need to obtain permission directly from the copyright holder.

Chapter 25
El Camino Sisyphus Style

En-route adventures and stunning landscapes along the real Camino have inspired books such as Paulo Coelho's *The Pilgrimage* [53], Hollywood movies *The Way* [54], and even award winning documentaries *Walking the Camino* [55]. As far as I know, nothing so lofty has come out of the virtual version and I think I know why.

My real-world route was dull, uneventful and it took me nowhere. It was a loop that started and finished at my home and ran along what once was a creek, but is now a concreted open stormwater drain, see Fig. 25.1.

Expectations were low that such a dull route could deliver the stimulus necessary for a pilgrimage. What is more, this time around my appearance blended with that of other walkers on the suburban trail. I was an undercover pilgrim doing a virtual pilgrimage. However, I still followed the two self-imposed rules of my analogue version, walk alone and no distractions.

As I looked for other routes to provide some relief from the monotony of my loop, *The Incline* popped into my head. The Incline is a short 1.42 km long, yet steep trail in Colorado, US, with a summit that is a staggering 610 m higher than the start, hence its nickname [56]. Walking up the Manitou Springs Incline one time is difficult, so why would anyone even consider doing it 690 times? [57]

If you are quick with numbers, you might have already worked out that walking up 610 m a total of 690 times gets you close to a figurative altitude of 421 km. If you are equally adept at trivia, you would know that this is the altitude of the International Space Station (ISS) orbit [58].

Walking up and down a hill just short of 700 times over the course of a year is absurd and meaningless. Similarly, climbing the same hill until one achieves the same elevation as the ISS, is still absurd, but meaningful because you will have figuratively reached a destination – and a very cool one for that matter. So why would someone walk the same hill more than 700 times, 719 times to be precise? One reason is to beat the guy that reached the ISS, another is more symbolic: 719 is the Area Code for Colorado Springs.

Fig. 25.1 Picture from El Camino de Santiago (top) and my stormwater drain Camino (bottom). (Top picture courtesy of Matthew and Heidi Smith)

Thinking about the absurd rivalry between two very fit guys searching for meaning in the Rocky Mountains allowed me to reframe my own predicament. I realised finding routes with more appeal than my stormwater drain would not make for a more meaningful pilgrimage.

I convinced myself to not only tolerate the mundane loops of my walk, but to also embrace them for what they were: another reminder of Sisyphus pushing his boulder up the *same* mountain, for eternity. So when you look at it that way, I wasn't just doing loops around my house, though that was exactly what I was doing, I was doing El Camino de Santiago Sisyphus style – and I loved it.

Adding meaning, if not purpose, to help people undertake routine tasks has not been overlooked by organisations who have rebranded the mundane as exciting. In lieu of going to the office every day, we are offered a chance to be a hero every day, see a clear path to success, engage in personal quest-based narratives and win prizes at work [59]. Such is the offering of a company using "*all the mechanisms and strategies that make games exciting and addictive to sustainably drive employee engagement, learning, and performance*" [59] an approach known as gamification.

The reason I think gamification works so well for those attempting a tough physical feat such as The Incline, or even walk the Camino online is the very same reason why I have reservations about its use in the workplace. Gamification can add meaning, even purpose, to otherwise meaningless tasks, but working at one's workplace (not necessarily the office, as we shall see) should be the equivalent of doing the El Camino de Santiago *in* Spain – no need for added gamification. And so, an important signpost on alignment:

> **29) Work which is aligned with its environment does not require added meaning.**

The use of gamification in the workplace might also suggest that work and tasks can not only be decoupled, as I had initially wondered, but that it might be inevitable.

It took me a good dose of meaningless and repetitive loops to arrive at a similar conclusion as the German sociologist and economist Max Weber reached in the early 1900s. Weber argued that to become more productive at a lower cost involves investigating every opportunity to make tasks more efficient [60]. This *rational efficiency* process, he noted, came at the expense of removing traditions, values, and emotions which were strong motivators within such activities.

Rational efficiency might well make an organisation more efficient, but conversely it could strip them naked. A compilation [61] of 30 of the most common rituals adopted by some organisations illustrates the process of re-introducing activities that may have fallen to this process. These include 'Grow Days' where employees are given a day off work to invest in upskilling, and 'Critical Thinking Starters' where meetings begin by asking a critical question.

Two signposts here are:

> **30) The pursuit of efficiencies might strip work of its meaning.**

> **31) The need of gamification and added rituals might be tell-tale signs of an overly efficient workplace.**

Weber had a lot more to say, eventually leading to his *Bureaucratic Management theory* [62]. Not long after, we would see the development of another management theory: Taylor's *Scientific Management* [63]. Both theories set expectations about how work should be done and managed and continue to shape the workplace over a century later.

Sisyphus' Backpack: Carrying the Workplace
I didn't pack anything for the virtual Camino. I had no need to carry clothes and with my warm bed nearby, I didn't need a sleeping bag or to struggle with a wet tent. Most definitely, I didn't need a backpack. This made me realise that the vast majority of the stuff that I carried to Sydney was intended to help progress the walk – with the exception of a notebook and a pen, which I packed for the pilgrimage itself.

Can we think about the workplace as a backpack, and consider its contents in relation to the role they play in supporting tasks (walking) and work (pilgrimage)?

I tried. But the clarity I had about the purpose of items I packed didn't follow to workplace components. That a fish tank can be the embodiment of work, makes things too difficult.

Still, it was an intriguing exercise that I invite you to try. Unpack the components in your workplace and assess whether they help you progress a task, support work, or both. You may find the *why* behind each decision is more interesting than the item itself. If like me, you might end up with a list of items supporting tasks, which make up a 'taskplace'; and another list, incredibly shorter, that makes a workplace.

At a time when many are questioning the purpose of the office, it might be best to offload the deadweight of items which add to a 'taskplace' and carry only those which make it a workplace.

As I uploaded my loop-earned kilometres into the website, I could see my virtual whereabouts being updated along the French route. Sometimes I had a look at the online map and I clicked on the street view to see the beautiful scenery that I virtually passed through and was left feeling a sense of joy, virtually. *Virtually* in both of its meanings: the computing of a simulation of the real world, and its other meaning of almost or nearly, but not completely, what it should be.

Open Access This chapter is licensed under the terms of the Creative Commons Attribution 4.0 International License (http://creativecommons.org/licenses/by/4.0/), which permits use, sharing, adaptation, distribution and reproduction in any medium or format, as long as you give appropriate credit to the original author(s) and the source, provide a link to the Creative Commons license and indicate if changes were made.

The images or other third party material in this chapter are included in the chapter's Creative Commons license, unless indicated otherwise in a credit line to the material. If material is not included in the chapter's Creative Commons license and your intended use is not permitted by statutory regulation or exceeds the permitted use, you will need to obtain permission directly from the copyright holder.

Chapter 26
Postcard from Pamplona

My Camino came with extras that were not included in the Sydney pilgrimage: I got postcards. One of these was from when I arrived at Pamplona and, allegedly, I had a go at running with the bulls. A postcard, or better said a digital image of a postcard, arrived by email each time I accumulated the number of kilometres that warranted one.

A great deal of attention was paid to recreating the necessary ornamental cues of a real-world postcard in the digital card. For example, stamps were of course unnecessary, but my digital postcard still had them, and they showed the imperfections that real stamps have, and the card was written using a computer font mimicking cursive handwriting. The card itself showed marks of wear and tear with tattered corners and scars from a long journey at the hands of international postal services.

My digital postcards were a *skeuomorphism,* a mouthful of a word for a simple but fascinating concept: to give an object (digital or analogue) the necessary properties of the original object it tries to represent. The goal is for the imitation to inherit the familiarity and evoke similar emotions as the original. This process requires knowledge of the key characteristics of the original object to appropriately convey essence, and then it must discover ways to transfer those into the new object.

Twelve years before I received my virtual postcard from Pamplona, I got on a plane and flew to the opposite side of the world. It was 2008, a time when disciplines like sociology, economics, you name it, had developed a peak interest in virtual worlds as a way to further their studies [64]. This interest was shared by architecture – after all, it's easier, faster, and cheaper to design, build, and maintain a building in a virtual world than the real world [65]. It wasn't long before organisations began experimenting with virtual environments for work related activities.

Amongst this hype I travelled to Manchester, UK, to study an early adopter of *Second Life*, a popular virtual world at the time. The organisation's real-world office featured rows of desks with a corridor along one side and windows along the other. All of this was sandwiched between a suspended acoustic tile ceiling and a grey carpet. In other words, a typical open plan office.

On the other hand, the company's *Second Life* workplace was a glass sphere floating over the sea, Fig. 26.1. The organisation's metaphorical consistency, in particular its real-world physics, was quite sophisticated. However, when it came to model the work environment, they mimicked its real-world equivalent as closely as they could – just like my postcard from Pamplona.

A floating glass sphere in the middle of the ocean? Not a problem. Interacting online in an environment that doesn't mimic the real world... well, that was problematic.

> *What I like about our [Virtual] office is that it is the opposite of replicating a real-world office, but still has very good functionality. It has meeting space and presentation areas. So there are some good practical office uses, within an innovative environment.* (Managing Director [1])

Virtual worlds struggled to shake off their gaming origins. They were seen as gimmicky and a very real digital apocalypse in 2012 wiped out many of them [66]. But some worlds survived, including *Second Life* which has revamped their virtual working offer under the slogan "*Remote Work Redefined*" [67].

Fig. 26.1 Sketch of Second Life office

A clear lesson from the pandemic was that regardless of the significantly improved interface of virtual worlds, remote work, or rather meetings, overwhelmingly moved to video conferencing platforms, not to virtual worlds.

> **Irving and the Metaverse**
> The initial excitement and hopes set upon virtual worlds of old are now being rebadged into the metaverse [68] and I am excited to see this new meta-skeuomorphism. But as we start to build new worlds and new versions of ourselves in them, I worry about what we might leave behind, in particular I'm concerned about Irving.
>
> When the Chicago-based Vienna Sausage Company moved to a new plant, their sausages lost their distinct red colour and signature snap [69]. The company retained the same recipe, ingredients, and process, but once they moved into a purposely designed, state-of-the-art new facility, their sausages came out pink and snap-less.
>
> They pondered their conundrum and finally remembered Irving, a well-loved employee who transported the sausages through the jumble of the old plant to the smoke house. The trip through the mazes of the previously unplanned facility allowed the sausages to cool and acquire their distinctive colour and consistency.
>
> *"The new plant had no jumbled maze. It was the very model of efficiency"*, reflected the Chairman of the Vienna Sausage Company [69].
>
> As we face opportunities to create new worlds of work in the Metaverse, or new configurations in the real world, we must be mindful not to leave behind 'Irvings' and other aspects of work that may seem inefficient but deliver competitive advantages.

Despite falling short in meeting their high expectations, virtual worlds left me searching for cues that communicate the essence of work – and produced another signpost:

32) Understanding work cues can help improve current and emerging work environments.

The outcome of this signpost would be a list of useful attributes of what makes a workplace. Useful no doubt, but also incomplete because of a shortcoming which goes back to the difficulty of defining what work is. This is so difficult that some, starting with Aristotle, found it easier to define work not by what it is, but by what it's not [70]. For example, work is that which is not leisure.

The point here is that an essential quality of a workplace is also what it is not – a point that it's also a signpost:

33) The workplace is also what it is not.

Therefore, the workplace needs not only to satisfy its own list of requirements, it must also manage those of other domains it might be in conflict with. Theories from work and family life-balance [71] suggest people have developed different ways to integrate, or segment, these two domains by creating, managing, and crossing the border. While some might work happily on a laptop at the dining table, others might not have walls at home thick enough, physically or metaphorically, to create the segmentation they need.

Engulfed in endless debates on the benefits of open plan office layouts, designers overlooked exploring the design implications of working from home (WFH), mostly reducing the topic to satisfying technical requirements of working at home: a fast Internet connection, a reliable video conferencing application, and a good file sharing system. However, these items support tasks, not work.

More importantly, the workplace (the place where people work) doesn't cease to exist when people stop going to the office and start working from home – if anything the workplace multiplies.

An assumption many make when thinking about the workplace is equating it with the office. However, the office is a relatively recent phenomenon in the history of work. An invention of sorts which came out of a complex economic, social and technology context [1, 72]. Historically, work was done elsewhere including homes; and even when offices were developing as places of work, some people still chose to WFH. For example, banking dynasties in the nineteenth century such as the Rothschilds and Barings opted to operate from luxurious homes [73], not to spare a commute, but to make their clients feel at ease.

The COVID-19 pandemic has given us the opportunity, if not responsibility, to consider home as a proper workplace – once again.

As soon as I entered the last kilometres of my virtual Camino, an email with digital certificates of completion arrived in three formats: square, portrait, and landscape. They were formatted to suit social media platforms so that I could "*show them off*" however I wanted. These certificates were a great skeuomorphism, they digitally communicated the essence of achievement from the tiered twirly embossed seals on fancy paper of old.

Open Access This chapter is licensed under the terms of the Creative Commons Attribution 4.0 International License (http://creativecommons.org/licenses/by/4.0/), which permits use, sharing, adaptation, distribution and reproduction in any medium or format, as long as you give appropriate credit to the original author(s) and the source, provide a link to the Creative Commons license and indicate if changes were made.

The images or other third party material in this chapter are included in the chapter's Creative Commons license, unless indicated otherwise in a credit line to the material. If material is not included in the chapter's Creative Commons license and your intended use is not permitted by statutory regulation or exceeds the permitted use, you will need to obtain permission directly from the copyright holder.

Chapter 27
66 loops

It took me 66 loops in the stormwater drain trail over the same number of days to complete the 774 km of El Camino online. A significantly slower pace when compared to the 905 km in 42 days of my walk to Sydney. However, this time around I didn't have to put my life on hold and I squeezed the pilgrimage in alongside my daily life and unescapable household chores.

> **Bookmark of Thoughts**
> A team of researchers [74] gave a list of words to scuba divers to memorise while they were on land and when they were under water. The divers recalled more words when quizzed in the same environment they memorised the words in. That is, their memory improved when tested at the learning environment compared to a different one – this is known as the *reinstatement effect*. I have mentioned this effect in workplace discussions, suggesting we design environments that provide cues to help workers remember things [75] – particularly relevant for gig-workers who change environments frequently.
>
> *Environmental context-dependent memory* is a fascinating field of research with its fair share of nuances and intricacies that are best left to proper studies [76] on the topic. But, reading, writing, or even talking about it, is not nearly as fun as experiencing it. And experienced it I did during my 66 loops.
>
> The best way I can explain it, is when you surprise yourself about recalling the words of a song you thought you would not remember, but when the time comes, the words come out. Scholars in the subject will be quick to point out the flaws of my analogy, but as I walked over and over my loop, I would surprise myself by remembering, on cue, what I was thinking about in that same spot a few laps ago; without even trying.
>
> My loop, that concreted stormwater drain, now serves as a trusty bookmark of thoughts.

No mental gymnastics could convince me that I had done the Camino de Santiago. Neither the three certificates or the postcards (or perhaps because I got postcards) could persuade me otherwise. Yet, as clear as I am about that, I am also certain that I didn't just walk, I really did do a pilgrimage.

This pilgrimage changed my mind about online pilgrimages, and I now feel more at ease with my iguana too – it just needs to be given a fair go.

The intangibility of this pilgrimage created signposts which leaned heavily towards the purpose, meaning and essence of work and the workplace. These might seem to be the domain of the many management and HR consultants, but these signposts should concern designers too. Why? Because *"one who knows the why, can bear almost any how"*. This might sound a bit too existentialist and better left for Viktor Frankl's Man's Search of Meaning [77] than a book on workplace design, but if slightly adjusted, its wisdom becomes very relevant: one who doesn't know the why, might not bear *any* how. When fleshed out a bit more this becomes our last and a very relevant signpost:

> **34) In the absence of work, with only tasks left to do, no workplace would suffice.**

Having learnt not to expect much out of the last step of a pilgrimage, I don't even know where I took it. What I did notice was that on the last email from the organisers, along with my certificates, there was a question: *"Ready to take on your next challenge?"* Beneath was a link to other virtual challenges they offered. I wasn't ready, but the challenge came anyway – and not from their link.

Open Access This chapter is licensed under the terms of the Creative Commons Attribution 4.0 International License (http://creativecommons.org/licenses/by/4.0/), which permits use, sharing, adaptation, distribution and reproduction in any medium or format, as long as you give appropriate credit to the original author(s) and the source, provide a link to the Creative Commons license and indicate if changes were made.

The images or other third party material in this chapter are included in the chapter's Creative Commons license, unless indicated otherwise in a credit line to the material. If material is not included in the chapter's Creative Commons license and your intended use is not permitted by statutory regulation or exceeds the permitted use, you will need to obtain permission directly from the copyright holder.

Part V
Laying Paths

Chapter 28
Following Signposts

What a journey it has been. Five years ago I would have had a hard time believing a commuter flight from Sydney to Melbourne would fill my mind with iguanas and send me on a pilgrimage.

Describing my pilgrimages as two round trips to the International Space Station (1679 km) tells only half of the story. The other half is best told by the signposts. The irony here is that after questioning if it really, really, mattered where we work, I now have 34 different ways to think about why it matters where we work.

Putting aside the sheer number of signposts, what stands out the most is how different they are from each other. They range from the way we exchange ideas, to existentialist commentary with a whole lot in between. Their variety becomes even more apparent when they are listed out as you will see in Appendix A: List of Signposts.

There is one other thing about these signposts.

They were not written retrospectively as enigmatic breadcrumbs leading to a place I had already found. I forego such literary licence because pilgrimages don't work that way and I wanted you to join me as a fellow pilgrim. I am as curious as you might be to find out where all these signposts lead.

*

Six months have passed, probably more.

For that long I have been searching to see where Signpost 2, the one which says that the workplace should promote absurdity, will take us. How does it work? Maybe a workplace that promotes absurdity doesn't work at all.

I have also tried to reach the final destination of the signpost about adversities promoting innovation, and the one on boredom as a thinking tool, and…well… I have tried to reach the destinations of all of them. After following their directions for months, I've reached a dead end and find myself at the spot where the trail ends and the signposts continue to point to the horizon.

I can't go any further, nor can I walk away. I have tried equally hard to find the answers or forget about the questions, but I can't.

The consequences of indulging in ever bigger questions about the workplace have caught up with me.

Eventually, I come across a seemingly frivolous distinction between trails and paths which turned out to be very useful in helping me find my way out of this dead end: trails extend backwards, paths extend forward [78]. To reach the destination of the many signposts I've created, I need to start laying paths from where the trails end.

Open Access This chapter is licensed under the terms of the Creative Commons Attribution 4.0 International License (http://creativecommons.org/licenses/by/4.0/), which permits use, sharing, adaptation, distribution and reproduction in any medium or format, as long as you give appropriate credit to the original author(s) and the source, provide a link to the Creative Commons license and indicate if changes were made.

The images or other third party material in this chapter are included in the chapter's Creative Commons license, unless indicated otherwise in a credit line to the material. If material is not included in the chapter's Creative Commons license and your intended use is not permitted by statutory regulation or exceeds the permitted use, you will need to obtain permission directly from the copyright holder.

Chapter 29
Fork on the Road

The chapters that follow are about the many trails I have covered and the paths I've started to lay to get closer to where the signposts point. I invite you to come along.

However, you might choose to find your own way and build your own paths from here. In such a case, go straight to Part VI and I'll meet you there.

Open Access This chapter is licensed under the terms of the Creative Commons Attribution 4.0 International License (http://creativecommons.org/licenses/by/4.0/), which permits use, sharing, adaptation, distribution and reproduction in any medium or format, as long as you give appropriate credit to the original author(s) and the source, provide a link to the Creative Commons license and indicate if changes were made.

The images or other third party material in this chapter are included in the chapter's Creative Commons license, unless indicated otherwise in a credit line to the material. If material is not included in the chapter's Creative Commons license and your intended use is not permitted by statutory regulation or exceeds the permitted use, you will need to obtain permission directly from the copyright holder.

Chapter 30
The Wisdom of the Locals

In preparing for my walk, I mapped the route all the way from Melbourne to Sydney and planned where I would stop and when. As it turned out, factors like the wind and rain, and even my mood (who knew?) didn't care about my well-intentioned plans.

Planning beyond a few days ahead became pointless, and every so often I found myself at a coffee shop with maps spread out on the table and my walking paraphernalia scattered around me. It was only a matter of time before a conversation started.

"Oh, yeah… you should be fine", I was told by helpful locals after showing them my route to the next town. At other times they would draw a line on my map and in a tone of sharing a secret tell me about a shortcut: "You will see a little dirt road (before / after) a (big tree / intersection), turn there." The wisdom of the locals took me along routes that I didn't know existed.

If I was ever to get to the figurative destination that my signposts were leading, it was clear I would benefit from this type of wisdom. To capture it, I asked people who are dispersed around the world to share their local knowledge in the fields of design, management, and technology.

You can meet our 22 Signpost locals in Appendix B: Meet the locals.

These chats were incredibly useful as well as marked a crucial point in time when I would let my iguana loose to roam in the wild, to be challenged, and continue to evolve in other 'islands'.

This process also allowed me to experience firsthand how machines are likely to support, rather than substitute for humans in the future. Where algorithms behind search engines were exceptional in finding relevant research on the many topics covered by the signposts (the known trails), the humans I interviewed, our locals, were extremely helpful in identifying opportunities to extend paths. A good

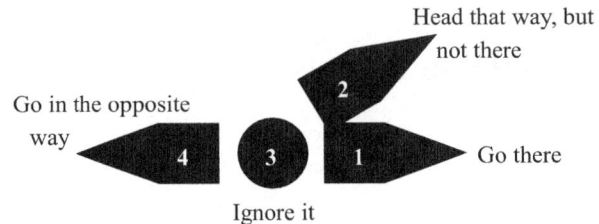

Fig. 30.1 Calibration of the signpost scale

example of combining the processing and storage systems of a machine with the human cognitive capability to solve fuzzy and uncertain problems [79].

To avoid overwhelming our locals with all the signposts, I chose to probe into only seven, the ones that I thought were the most representative. These were:

- **Signpost 1:** Exchanging ideas too early and too often hinders their diversity and potential to innovate.
- **Signpost 2:** The workplace should promote absurdity.
- **Signpost 4:** Adversities are worth keeping, even introduced, in the workplace to promote innovation.
- **Signpost 6:** Boredom can become a useful thinking tool.
- **Signpost 11:** The process of designing a workplace can get in the way of creating an environment which meets its purpose.
- **Signpost 25:** Work and tasks are different yet interconnected.
- **Signpost 30:** The pursuit of efficiencies might strip work of its meaning.

These were so elusive that I not only asked for directions to get there, but also if it was a good idea to follow them at all. The locals helped me calibrate the selected signposts by indicating the direction they would take compared to the direction the signpost pointed. I gave them four options, Fig. 30.1.

If they said:

1) **Go there:** meant they agreed with the premise of the signpost and felt it worthwhile to continue exploring in that direction.
2) **Head that way, but not there:** something along the lines of "yes, but…", an agreement with an objection that results in a different destination.
3) **Ignore it:** the premise is irrelevant, or should not be thought about in that way.
4) **Go in the opposite direction:** disagreement with the premise and a suggestion to go the opposite way.

Open Access This chapter is licensed under the terms of the Creative Commons Attribution 4.0 International License (http://creativecommons.org/licenses/by/4.0/), which permits use, sharing, adaptation, distribution and reproduction in any medium or format, as long as you give appropriate credit to the original author(s) and the source, provide a link to the Creative Commons license and indicate if changes were made.

The images or other third party material in this chapter are included in the chapter's Creative Commons license, unless indicated otherwise in a credit line to the material. If material is not included in the chapter's Creative Commons license and your intended use is not permitted by statutory regulation or exceeds the permitted use, you will need to obtain permission directly from the copyright holder.

Chapter 31
Let's Go!

In a nutshell, the calibrations tell us to continue to follow the signposts, the details can be found in Appendix C: Signpost calibration.

But before we set off for *there*, I asked our locals to re-calibrate the same signposts, but this time according to what they perceived to be the established point of view. That is, not based on what they would do, but what they thought the industry or sector in which they operate would do.

If we follow the established view calibration, we are more likely to head in the opposite direction or do nothing at all.

Figure 31.1 shows these two opposing results depending on the viewpoint. The area of the shapes is proportional to the percentages of responses.

The results of these calibrations illustrate the tension between the established view and the personal view. They also show the push and pull that I experienced for months on end, with the signposts simultaneously luring me to go there but also to head in the opposite direction.

Then Ethan warned me, "the established view is tricky, because as you know, academics don't agree". Well, 'Ethan' is not his real name, all of our locals were given pseudonyms. But what he was telling me was that the established point of view doesn't imply a consensus in academia, nor in the industry as Brooke also warned, "the established view really depends on the type of client."

Even if taken with a pinch of salt, this view is still important because it reflects the ways in which organisations have overcome challenges in the past. At the same time, it's important to know the extent to which the circumstances and assumptions behind this view are still relevant – or is it established just because that's the way it is?

Along the walk I received less advice from fewer locals and still made it to Sydney, but some might question whether a group of 22 people, the number of experts I interviewed, is too small to have valid statistical significance. They would be right, it doesn't. I would have to be able to demonstrate that if the study is to be

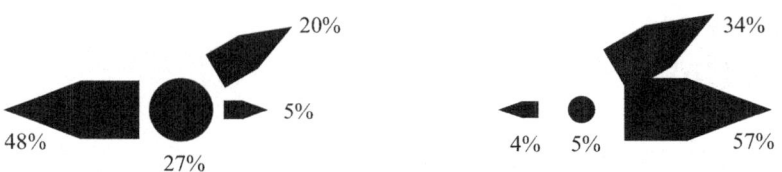

Fig. 31.1 Calibration of the seven selected signposts by all 22 local participants. Established view (left), Personal view (right)

(hypothetically) repeated 100 times, it would produce the same result at least 95 times. For that to happen a larger sample and a different sampling technique are required.

However, that doesn't mean that the calibrations are wrong or that they can't be used, far from it. Talking to a small group allows us to analyse the reasons behind the calibrations in greater detail. In addition, even with the right number of people for statistical analysis, the calibrations would neither prove, nor disprove, the signposts. Other methods are needed for that.

Open Access This chapter is licensed under the terms of the Creative Commons Attribution 4.0 International License (http://creativecommons.org/licenses/by/4.0/), which permits use, sharing, adaptation, distribution and reproduction in any medium or format, as long as you give appropriate credit to the original author(s) and the source, provide a link to the Creative Commons license and indicate if changes were made.

The images or other third party material in this chapter are included in the chapter's Creative Commons license, unless indicated otherwise in a credit line to the material. If material is not included in the chapter's Creative Commons license and your intended use is not permitted by statutory regulation or exceeds the permitted use, you will need to obtain permission directly from the copyright holder.

Chapter 32

Your Armchair Pilgrimage

> I am changing my answer on boredom, I think you should actually go for that one. I will be processing it obsessively for some time, I assure you.

So read the message from Nora to let me know she had changed her mind. Nora didn't walk with me to Sydney, but still experienced similar effects with the signposts. I received other messages from locals who also embarked on mini pilgrimages following signposts in their own minds.

Any lingering doubts I had on whether one could deconstruct a pilgrimage from its walk vanished. Still unsure? Hear it from Rev. Robert Willis, Dean of Canterbury Cathedral, who knows a thing or two about pilgrimages:

> *You could journey all around the world on foot and not be a pilgrim because your heart and mind are not open to the insights… and maybe you haven't had the conversations which will shock you… from the most strange people. On the other hand, you could be… at home and be a pilgrim in heart and mind…So,* [a pilgrimage] *is not about physical movement, though that's the icon of it.* [80]

After reading this far and reflecting on the conversations I had with unlikely people along the way, you may be feeling prepared to open your mind and join me as a fellow pilgrim following signposts. When in doubt, just remember: a tourist is interested in seeing the sights, the pilgrim is interested in having insights [80].

Open Access This chapter is licensed under the terms of the Creative Commons Attribution 4.0 International License (http://creativecommons.org/licenses/by/4.0/), which permits use, sharing, adaptation, distribution and reproduction in any medium or format, as long as you give appropriate credit to the original author(s) and the source, provide a link to the Creative Commons license and indicate if changes were made.

The images or other third party material in this chapter are included in the chapter's Creative Commons license, unless indicated otherwise in a credit line to the material. If material is not included in the chapter's Creative Commons license and your intended use is not permitted by statutory regulation or exceeds the permitted use, you will need to obtain permission directly from the copyright holder.

© The Author(s) 2022
A. Chevez, *The Pilgrim's Guide to the Workplace*, SpringerBriefs in Business,
https://doi.org/10.1007/978-981-19-4759-9_32

Chapter 33
On Wilderness, Carnivals, and Foolishness

Let's start our pilgrimage by following one of the most significant signposts of all: the workplace should promote absurdity. Signpost 2 came out of the idea that our capability to be absurd gives us a competitive edge over logic-based algorithms in the future of work. Because of this, absurdity should be nurtured at the places where we work (Signpost 3).

But the long-standing relationship between rationality and the workplace cannot be underestimated, so we must follow this signpost with caution. In spite of my concerns, the calibrations tell a different story. Almost all of our locals wanted to at least head that way, with the majority willing to go there, see righthand chart of Fig. 33.1.

In light of what you now know about these calibrations, the percentages are unnecessary, simply pay attention to the size of the shapes. Any difficulties in distinguishing small differences between them can be taken as a visual representation of the margin of error.

I was surprised by the established view (lefthand chart), in which a larger portion of the calibrations point towards where the signpost is pointing rather than in the opposite direction.

"There is room for absurdity in the workplace", said Brooke and then went on to explain the variety of rooms in the workplace, such as 'innovation labs', and other creative spaces where absurdity could exist. It soon became apparent that the agreement with this signpost had to do with the perceived association of absurdity with creativity. However, Brooke continued:

> I don't see absurdity as a sort of wholesale, you know, a thing that takes over the whole of the workplace. The problem is how you can continue to get the benefit out of that experience when people leave that space.

Fig. 33.1 Calibration of Signpost 2 – absurdity. Established view (left), Personal view (right)

And that is where that trail ends, and the questions start. Can absurdity be contained behind doors, in a room? And what about other aspects of absurdity beyond that of being a steppingstone to creativity? Claire said:

> Absurdity is big and powerful, it has something very pure to it, and maybe it's not even possible for the workplace to promote absurdity. Maybe we ignore it and don't make it a destination. Absurdity will find its way. It is rationality which creates absurdity.

"It is rationality which creates absurdity"… mmm, hold that thought.

In his paper *The trouble with wilderness* [81], William Cronon, Professor of history, geography, and environmental studies, puts forward an interesting idea: wilderness is a product of civilisation. In other words, it was not until we developed civilisation that we positioned nature as wilderness. Cronon then attributes much of our dysfunctional relationship with nature to this idea of wilderness.

In a similar way, our dysfunctional relationship with absurdity might come from conceiving it as a by-product of our rationality. However, our signpost is a bit trickier than the wilderness-civilisation dichotomy because we cannot explore the world of the absurd as easily as getting into a car and heading off to the woods. Or so I thought. Our local Gavin sent me on a path:

> Check out carnivals. Carnivals are little moments where people are allowed to be absurd. You know, when in medieval times the king dressed up as a peasant and the peasant dressed up as a king and everyone reverses their roles. But it's only for a day or so, once a year, that you can upset the balance of everything.

Gavin was talking about the *Carnivalesque world* [82] as described by Russian linguistic and literary critic Mikhail Bakhtin. Gavin continued:

> But more than anarchy or a safety valve for releasing societal tensions, the carnival creates the potential for negotiating new relationships.

Before I knew it, I was deep into the carnival trails. A world of absurdity which is not only void of hierarchy and normality, but also one which cannot be contemplated, but lived for as long as the laws of "*the reverse side of the world*" are in effect [83].

I then realised that I had seen a similar type of absurdity in some workplaces before, but not within the walls of colourful rooms with funky chairs and lots of sticky notes on the walls. It was at the end of the work week when hierarchies are temporarily flattened during Friday's afterwork drinks, not by employees putting on masks as in carnivals, but by removing them and mingling as people.

The trails of the wilderness and carnivals revealed the richness of absurdity which sits behind Signpost 2 as well as the one which creates new meaning and purpose in Signpost 13, and also Signpost 14 (seeing normality through absurdity can show the absurd as normal); and 15 (normality can be the offspring of the unchallenged).

In this type of absurdity, we have no choice but to see the world differently, albeit temporarily. And while exploring these trails, I came across a study [84] that singles out a type of environment which *"activates a different mindset"* and makes us *"seek novelty and unconventional routes."* This wonderful environment is a disorderly environment.

According to the study, disorderly environments can help people to *"break away from tradition, order and convention"* and so the researchers advise against what they called minimalist design trends and desk sharing because these can reduce the opportunities to make a mess.

I wondered if the explorations of the absurd in architectural movements like postmodernism (see BEST stores designed by SITE in the US during the 70s [85]), or even deconstructivism could produce the same results as a messy desk or room can. I couldn't find evidence of that. But according to Gavin these types of designs are only expressions of absurdity; and in the end, the few buildings that are actually built, still function as a big box.

Then came my chat with Miles. With the assertiveness of those who drew a line on my map to Sydney, he said: *"check out James March and The Technology of Foolishness. March was an absolute genius!"*

With that title and such recommendation how could I not? March's *Technology of Foolishness* (ToF) [86] is a fascinating essay which speculates on ways in which we can escape the fettering logic of our reason. One of these ways is play, which March defines as the *"deliberate, temporary relaxation of rules in order to explore the possibilities of alternative rules."*

March was not only a genius, but brave too. He dared to make a case for taboo concepts like coercion and hypocrisy in organisations and society. In the case of hypocrisy, March interprets it as the inconsistency between expressed values and behaviour and thus *"a bad man with good intentions may be a man experimenting with the possibility of becoming good."* I now think about an organisation which fails to live up to their values as one experimenting with the possibility of becoming better.

March even found a way in which we can act within the system of reason and still do things that are foolish. It's incredibly simple and you can try it: forget things. In ToF, memory is an enemy.

March published his ToF in the early 70s and I couldn't wait to find out what type of innovations or organisations it has prompted since. I couldn't believe my luck when I came across a paper entitled: *Whatever happened to "The Technology of Foolishness?"* [87], but I was quickly disappointed. I learnt that while the ToF has been much praised, it has not been much used; and when it has, it has been mostly in a superficial and ritualistic manner with some of March's key ideas sugar-coated.

To be fair, the ToF is far from being plug-and-play and as much as it is thought provoking, it gives no advice on how it can be installed in organisations.

Continuing down this trail we eventually bump into Richard Farson's *Management of the Absurd* [88]. Farson is quick to differentiate absurdity from stupidity (a synonym of foolishness), but rather than trying to pick a fight with March's ideas, I think it's Farson's way to make peace with our dysfunctional relationship with absurdity as a consequence of rationality. Farson's focus is on paradoxes, yet another layer of absurdity. One example is *"the better things are, the worse they feel"* which has striking similarities with our own Signpost 4 about adversities.

Continuing further down this trail, we see a growing interest in the role of paradoxes in management. In the book fittingly titled *Paradox Management* [89], we learn about the close relationship between how organisations respond to paradoxes and the value they create: better management of paradoxes, better organisations. Yet again, this type of absurdity seems different. It is more prevalent, persistent, and unavoidable than that of the altered world which we can only venture temporarily.

If from where we are now, we were to take out a pair of binoculars and point them backwards, we would see the trails of absurdism. There, life is absurd, not in itself, but in our absurd attempts to find meaning in it. But we won't go that far back. However, those up for a hike might want to check out Albert Camus' *The Myth of Sisyphus* [90].

Here we take a left turn and venture into the last trail on this signpost: Dadaism – an art movement which rejected logic and reason in favour of irrationality and nonsense. An example is Kurt Schwitters' *Environments in Constant Flow* [91], in which a column of debris would appear one day, and a grotto would appear on the next. This is as close as Dadaism got to architecture, but there is no Dadaist architecture as such, how can one build upon absurdity?

Instead, try this little exercise: cut words out of a newspaper (or any other text), put them in a hat and shake it, then take the words out one by one and write them down in the order in which they came out.

Voila! You are *"a writer, infinitely original and endowed with a sensibility that is charming though beyond the understanding of the vulgar"* [92] said Tristan Tzara, who came up with this method to create Dadaist poems.

It's such a simple and elegant way of creating new meaning through absurdity that I tried quite tenaciously to use it as a means of infusing absurdity into this book. But I couldn't.

Except for the rare occasion in which the words come out in the same order as the original text, its output is beyond the understanding of anyone, vulgar or not. Giving up on my writing style was easier than facing the possibility that Signpost 2, the landmark of my pilgrimage, took us nowhere. Then came this from the same local who introduced me to *The Technology of Foolishness*, Miles said:

> Innovation is an important purpose of an organisation, but I would not promote absurdity in 90% of the jobs that they perform.

I immediately recognised the brevity and temporary disruption of the world. Miles continued:

> Organisations need absence of absurdity to deliver what they do, to complete the tasks. There's no space for absurdity when we're talking about coordination.

Voila!

Tzara didn't care about coordination, the subjectivity of artistic outputs rarely do, but an organisation where no one understands each other would not go very far. The temporary exploration of the absurd needs to be followed by a much longer effort of rational coordination, free of nonsense.

I wondered, if I were an organisation, what percentage of time had I spent exploring the absurd? The result: 7% (42 days) of absurdity walking to Sydney and 93% trying to coordinate such absurdity as clearly as possible by reading, talking to others, and writing this book.

> **In Between 7% and 93%: A Lost Language**
>
> In *Madness and Civilisation* [93] the French philosopher Michel Foucault reflects on the changing nature of what insanity is and the different ways in which civilisation has dealt with it through time.
>
> In the Renaissance, insane people were part of society and there was a place for them to interact intellectually with reasonable people because they possessed *"knowledge of the limits of the world."* That would all change in what Foucault refers to as the Modern Era (eighteenth century) when *"Modern man no longer communicates with the madman ... There is no common language, or rather, it no longer exists."*
>
> I wonder if *The Technology of Foolishness*, *The Management of the absurd*, and *Paradox management*, aim to reinstate that lost common language which sits in between the seven percent of the time exploring the limits of the world and the 93% of the time to get there.

However, percentages do not imply importance. And so, be it through Friday night drinks, forgetting things, or good old messiness, the workplace should allow for opportunities to briefly venture into a different way of seeing the world. There lies the opportunity to go from logic-based innovations which lead to doing the same things we currently do cheaper and faster, to innovations that deliver unimaginable futures.

Once seen, the environment should promote the coordination of the absurd and make the most of the unavoidable paradoxes to arrive at such futures.

Open Access This chapter is licensed under the terms of the Creative Commons Attribution 4.0 International License (http://creativecommons.org/licenses/by/4.0/), which permits use, sharing, adaptation, distribution and reproduction in any medium or format, as long as you give appropriate credit to the original author(s) and the source, provide a link to the Creative Commons license and indicate if changes were made.

The images or other third party material in this chapter are included in the chapter's Creative Commons license, unless indicated otherwise in a credit line to the material. If material is not included in the chapter's Creative Commons license and your intended use is not permitted by statutory regulation or exceeds the permitted use, you will need to obtain permission directly from the copyright holder.

Chapter 34

The Art of Timing and Balance

> The moment you ask for two opinions on something new and interesting that you are doing, it will end up as a watered-down version.

Said Ron while calibrating Signpost 1: Exchanging ideas too early and too often hinders their diversity and potential to innovate.

With Ethan I talked about the various social processes that an idea and the person who comes up with it are exposed to the very moment they decide to share it:

> People will probably tell you: 'that's a nice idea, but have you thought about all the difficulties', or 'it has been tried and failed'.

March's ability to forget could be a practical solution here. Ethan added, "at the early stages an idea is very vulnerable and can die easily."

Henry saw things differently. For him, the experiences of others "stretches your imagination" and so exchanging ideas early and frequently is a good thing to do.

Claire told me that it's not so much about how early or often we share ideas, but about who we share them with: "the trust in the relationship predetermines what will happen to the idea." Though, she later reflected that while trust might allow the idea to develop, it might not contribute to, nor maintain, its uniqueness.

For Frank it was the type of 'tie' in the relationship which contributes to its novelty. In social networks, a strong tie develops when you interact with someone frequently. Frank explained:

> In a strong tie, what you know and what they know overlaps a lot, and you're more likely to have a similar worldview. But people who are far away in your social network, those which you don't interact much with (weak ties) are less likely to know the same things and more likely to know information which is new to you.

An intriguing example of how interacting with weak ties can promote innovation came during my chat with Kevin where we discussed a study [94] by an economics professor who found that during the alcohol prohibition era in the US there were 8–18% fewer patents in the counties which were under such prohibition law. Less informal interaction at bars, fewer patents.

The researcher then noted that as people rebuilt their networks, they connected with different individuals which in turn lead to new patents in different areas. The study concluded that *"while prohibition had a temporary effect on the rate of invention, it had a lasting effect on the direction of inventive activity"* [94] – innovation through weak ties.

Miles then told me that he agrees with the 'too early, too often' part of the signpost and backed it up with a study [95] which measured a decline in the quality of solutions in group settings. The study suggests that:

> *Organisations should be redesigned to intermittently isolate people from each other's work for best collective performance in solving complex problems.*

That conclusion is so, so very, close to our signpost that I was tempted to put my feet up and call it *the* destination of Signpost 1. However, Miles also told me that "we overestimate the value of a novel idea compared to a highly effective idea." Innovation, he argued, can benefit more from an integrated idea than a diverse one and added:

> If we consider innovation as building a product that would have a market success, then novelty on its own is not sufficient.

I heard this too from those at the cold front of delivering ideas, or as Quinn called it "the entrepreneurial approach to ideas", where the value proposition of the idea needs to be identified almost immediately, quickly followed by the development of a business model. A monumental task that requires early and frequent interactions.

With Alice I talked about brainstorming, which I believe takes us in the opposite direction of this signpost, but Alice identified 'time' as a key shared ingredient in both my pilgrimage and brainstorming used to arrive at a good idea.

> In brainstorming you start with all the standard, 'bad' ideas, but with time, the group runs out of these and starts to build on previous ones and new and better ideas start to come up.

For Uriel it wasn't about what had been discussed, but about what we share – the idea itself. Not a single part of Signpost 1 was spared. For Uriel:

> The issue is that we share ideas which don't come from a point of diversity. We tend to share ideas that don't look far enough.

Then Julia, a self-confessed extrovert, told me:

> My best ideas come from talking to other people and I share them as quickly as I can. This is my natural way of being and I haven't stop to think whether that was helping or hurting [the quality of the idea].

That is a short summary of key points from half of the locals that I interviewed. You might recognise some aspects of how you deal with your own and other peoples' ideas – or you might have a completely different take on Signpost 1. The myriad ways of approaching this signpost were reflected in its calibration. The personal point of view (righthand) had the largest "yes, but…" of all, see Fig. 34.1. And no one thought it was something we should ignore – no circle.

Fig. 34.1 Calibration of Signpost 1 – exchange of ideas. Established view (left), Personal view (right)

On the other hand, the established view (lefthand chart) is very different and equally important to understand. Claire nicely summarised this stark difference:

> The common belief is that collaboration is good for innovation. The earlier and the more often you exchange ideas, the better.

Indeed, many human endeavours – from teams and organisations to crowds and democracies – rely on solving problems collectively [95]. To this end, workplace designers put a lot of effort into creating environments which bring people together. Unsurprisingly, no other issue in the design of workplaces has received more attention than walls to connect (or buffer) workers from each other [96] – with the ensuing passionate debates on open vs enclosed floor plans.

As passionate as those debates are, so too are those on interacting too much. Researchers [97, 98] talk about the undesirable side effects that unrestrained collaboration can create in the workflow of organisations. An example of this is 'escalating citizenship', whereby collaborators can become institutional bottlenecks and work does not progress until they have had their say.

Others, like occupational psychologist Adrian Furnham, argue that:

> *Research shows unequivocally that brainstorming groups produce fewer and poorer quality ideas than the same number of individuals working alone.* [99]

In her book *Quiet: The power of introverts in a world that can't stop talking* [100], Susan Cain strings together a broad discussion on the shortcomings of collective thinking and she might have part of the answer when she argues that it's the social glue, as opposed to creativity which is the main benefit of group interaction.

Quiet was a very influential book, it gave a voice to the introverts in the workplace (an environment which favours the extrovert) and it didn't take long for a global furniture manufacturer to develop the, wait for it… *Susan Cain Quiet Spaces* [101]. This beautifully crafted range of personal environments with frosted glass and acoustic insulation is a practical way to support introspection and Signpost 1.

But here we reach an intersection with other signposts, including number 5: Aloneness needs to be within the ideal conditions of its effects on us (solitude) and the quality of the idea itself. At one point, ideas benefit from being shared and coordinated. But that would take us through another set of trails. We will not follow these and in Chap. 36 All Roads Lead to Rome I will explain why this is not a problem.

Open Access This chapter is licensed under the terms of the Creative Commons Attribution 4.0 International License (http://creativecommons.org/licenses/by/4.0/), which permits use, sharing, adaptation, distribution and reproduction in any medium or format, as long as you give appropriate credit to the original author(s) and the source, provide a link to the Creative Commons license and indicate if changes were made.

The images or other third party material in this chapter are included in the chapter's Creative Commons license, unless indicated otherwise in a credit line to the material. If material is not included in the chapter's Creative Commons license and your intended use is not permitted by statutory regulation or exceeds the permitted use, you will need to obtain permission directly from the copyright holder.

Chapter 35
The Trails and Territories of Adversity

The good things which belong to prosperity are to be wished; but the good things that belong to adversity are to be admired. - Francis Bacon, on Seneca [102]

I find Signpost 4 particularly intriguing. It tells us that adversities are worth keeping, even introduced, in the workplace to promote innovation. This signpost points in the opposite direction from the way in which design deals with adversity and David summarised this well:

> Architecture has a gene of optimism and utopia in it, we use architecture to 'show the better'.

This better version of the world has a lot to do with removing the bad, including adversity. That is why even if adversity is as good at delivering wisdom and innovation, design might be as hardwired to avoid it as the rest of us. Then Frank reminded me why it's important to follow Signpost 4:

> You read stories of people that worked for Steve Jobs and it sounds a lot like what you called 'Type 2 fun' – it was difficult at the time, but they look back on it with satisfaction and pride. And I wonder if we focus too much on Type 1 fun in the workplace – we want free food and massage chairs, which make people happy in the short-term but perhaps doesn't lead to lasting satisfaction. Perhaps the best work is a type of pilgrimage.

This signpost was the most polarising of the seven I discussed with our locals. Still, most of them agreed that existing adversities, the ones which come with the environment, have little to offer and are best removed. This is reflected in the calibrations where our locals separately adjusted keeping adversities and introducing them, Fig. 35.1. Note the bigger 'go there' arrow for introduced adversity (bottom, right).

All in all, when keep and introduced adversities are combined, the locals considered that we should still 'go there' – so let's go there.

This signpost covers a variety of knowledge domains which makes it easy to get lost. Fortunately for us, while knowledge is invisible it can be mapped [103, 104] and I have prepared a knowledge map of the territories that we will be passing through to help keep us out of trouble, see Fig. 35.2. However, this map doesn't aim to be a comprehensive one – such a map would confuse us more. Instead, it's a simplified and stylised version based on two academic journal databases (*Web of*

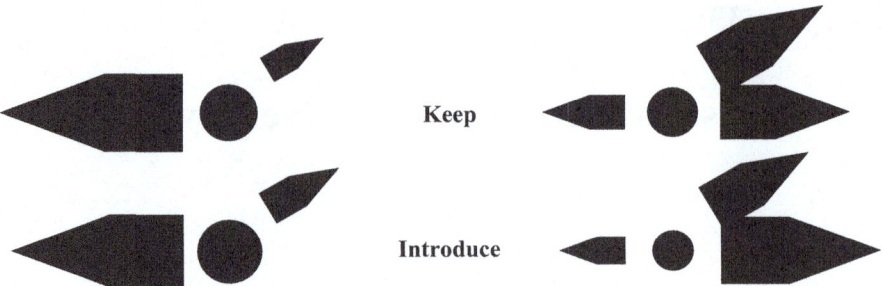

Fig. 35.1 Calibration of Signpost 4 – adversity. Established view (left), Personal view (right). Keep adversity (top), Introduce adversity (bottom)

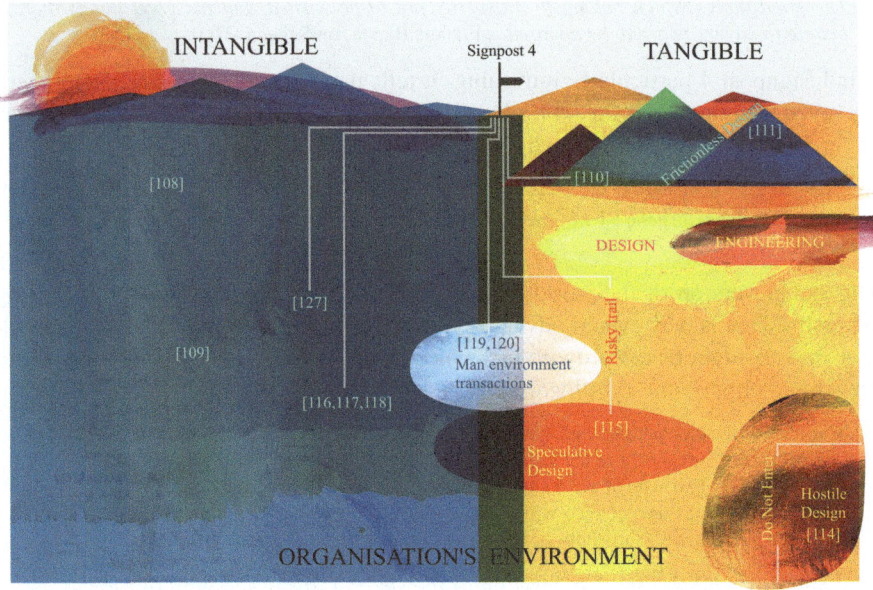

Fig. 35.2 Knowledge map of adversity in the workplace. The number in brackets indicates reference number

Science [105] and *Google Scholar* [106]) and the online tool *Open Knowledge Maps* [107].

The map focuses on two environments in which adversity occurs in organisations: intangible and tangible, represented in the western and eastern territories, respectively.

In the western territory, adversity finds its way through organisational culture and other intangible environments. For example, breaking the implicit agreement about the obligations that the employer bears toward employees (psychological contract) is considered a source of adversity [108]. Researchers found humour, laughing it off, to be a good way to manage this type of adversity. Overall, adversity occurring in intangible environments is mostly dealt with through resilience.

In the east, adversity occurs in tangible parameters from the physical environment in the workplace like temperature and illumination. This type of adversity is overcome through good design.

You might notice that the intangible territory is bigger than the tangible one. This is because disciplines studying this environment, like management, seem to be more curious about adversity than their counterparts studying tangible environments, like design and engineering.

One example from the intangible territory is the paper *Predicting Scientific Creativity: The role of adversity, collaborations, and work strategies* [109]. Here, the researchers position the adversity faced by scientists alongside the contemporary darling of the workplace: collaboration. Although this study didn't find adversity to be a predictor of scientific creativity, the question was asked. These questions are much rarer in tangible environments.

In workplace design adversity is almost always understood as lack of comfort. Here we find fringe studies reporting increased productivity under uncomfortable conditions, for example when it is uncomfortably cold [110]. The overwhelming conclusion from this territory is that adversity, better said discomfort, in the workplace is undesirable and must be eliminated. The extent to which this happens is taken as an indicator of the quality of the design.

There are numerous 'quality peaks' that can be reached by a combination of design and engineering trails. Let's explore one of these peaks: Frictionless Design.

In *The Design of Everyday Things* [111] Don Norman, cognitive scientist and usability engineer, makes a convincing case to use design to effortlessly guide the user through the function of an object, from stovetops to websites. Soon enough these principles found their way into the 'frictionless workplace' [112]: *"a workplace where tasks, policies, procedures, and structures are free of unnecessary effort,* [and] *undue stress... Achieving a frictionless workplace is the pinnacle of a great employee experience"* [113].

It is under this context that I found it extraordinary to encounter designers among our locals who not only saw value in adversity, but who, like Isabel, told me "[Signpost 4] is a number one for me. I have a strong view on purposeful friction."

But even if we agree, how do we use design to benefit from adversity? At the valley southeast of the peaks in our knowledge map, we find a type of design which actually puts adversity and discomfort into practice. Aptly it is called 'hostile design' and you might be more familiar with it than you think. One example is the middle armrest on benches to prevent rough sleepers from laying down on park benches.

The purpose of hostile design is to restrict behaviour and exclude particular people [114], not to innovate. I heard it loud and clear from the interviewees that adversity should never be used to alienate or exclude anyone in any environment. Olivia was particularly clear:

> I would definitely agree with [the use of adversity], it's just a question of what kind. If you said, well, we're going to make it harder for women to be promoted, then no!

With no other practical way in which design deals with adversity, we are left with one more region in this territory: speculative design. A good example of this is *Design Noir* [115] which explores the role of danger, adventure, and transgression in manufactured environments. These art-based propositions are valuable in their commentary and capacity to provoke thinking, but they are risky because it's unclear how they can contribute to organisations in the way Signpost 4 suggests. They might produce a décor which conveys the concept, but such a look might be left behind at the next office renovation because it failed to deliver its purpose.

As I was wandering rather aimlessly through the speculative trails, Ethan told me:

> If [employees] have less resources, they don't waste them. They think harder, they become more resourceful. Being resource constrained might be a good thing for innovation. Have a look at studies on organisational slack.

The organisational slack trail turned into a path to Signpost 4. From the many definitions on organisational slack, we will go here with *"the resources in or available to an organisation that are in excess of the minimum necessary to produce a given level of organisational output"* [116].

The first assumptions on organisational slack were that organisations with an excess of time, people, and money were better placed to innovate [117]. However, later studies [118] showed that organisations suffering from a lack of resources have higher levels of innovation, and that too much slack can be counterproductive. The most recent assumption is that *"zero slack leaves the organisation too inflexible, while too much slack results in inefficiencies accelerating the organisations' termination"* [116].

You may have already started making some connections here, but we will need more tiles to start laying our path. One of which comes from the notion of 'environmental press' which itself comes from a larger theory of *Man-Environment Transaction* [119]. It's really easy to get lost here, so we will just have a short peek into this trail. An environmental press is built on the crucial role that adaptation plays in how we relate to the environment. A situation in which an environmental press is above the competency of the person is not good, but too little is not good either.

Both, an environmental press and organisational slack advocate for environments, tangible and intangible, which are challenging enough.

The wider theory of Man-Environment Transaction also tells us that we are usually at adaptation level with respect to our environment and thus we filter out cognition of our physical surrounding [120]. But by purposefully altering our surroundings we could reignite the adaptation process. In words of Architect Peter Eisenman: *"The architecture we remember is that which never consoles or comfort us"* [121].

From where we are now, we can see at a distance the faint trail of environmental enrichment. This is a trail of interest because it's about stimulating the brain by enhancing cognitive and physical environments with puzzles and obstacles [122]. In other words, it is about making things purposely harder for a better quality of life.

However, environmental enrichment focuses on non-human primates and other animals kept in captivity. That is why it's not in our map and we will not spend time there.

Instead, we will have a short stroll through trails which make a bestselling book out of adversity– and we can certainly learn from that. Here is where we find books like *The Comfort Crisis* [123] and *Can't Hurt Me* [124] reminding us that we are too comfortable for our own good. Nothing new here, but common to both books is their use of gruelling physical experiences to reclaim the lost benefits of adversity.

Followers of the *Can't Hurt Me* way of life use hashtags like *#embracethesuck* and *#dontgetcomfortable* while posting pictures of themselves doing harrowing physical activities in pursuit of a better self. There are hundreds of thousands of posts in Instagram with these hashtags which remind me of times during my walk to Sydney, but then again, I was embracing so much suck that I didn't even think of taking a picture.

In *The Comfort Crisis* I learnt about Harvard-trained physician, Dr. Marcus Elliot, a proponent of taxing physical challenges known as misogi – referencing the old Japanese Shinto ritual of washing the body under a freezing cold waterfall, in winter. Following Dr. Elliot's trail, I came across a conversation he had with a global accounting firm [125] in which he shared the two rules he uses to set the level of difficulty of his misogi challenges: Rule one, if you do everything right, you should have just about 50% chance of completing the challenge. Rule two, don't die.

Ok… So how are these challenges supposed to help? Dr. Elliot explains this in a way which summarises the reliance of both books on tough physical challenges:

> *You're watching yourself do so much more than you ever dreamed you could, and you generalise from there. You start trusting that you can do much more than you thought possible in other situations.* [125]

The suggestion that we build confidence from experience has been long explored and formalised by psychologist Albert Bandura in his *Self-Efficacy Theory* (SET) [126]. The challenge here is to determine the extent that toughing it out outside the office can lead to knowledge workers innovating within the organisation. In SET competency is built across similarly associated tasks.

Fortunately, we don't have to worry about that, nor follow this trail any further. Our signpost argues that the adversities should come from the workplace itself, not from a weekend challenge. Still, this trail has shown us that adversity can be made approachable and even popular. Key here is to design a sort of adversity on tap, one which can be controlled in its intensity, opted in, and opted out, even bragged about – just like physical challenges. This ability to control adversity was stressed by our locals as a pre-requisite for where conversations about this signpost could begin.

We have embarked on a long expedition following this signpost, fortunately there is just one last trail to cover. This trail is important because it tells us that as things get better, we become fussier. Participants in an experiment [127] were shown a series of dots that varied in colour from very purple to very blue and were asked to say whether the dot was blue or not. The researchers then decreased the frequency of blue dots. Surprisingly, the participants' concept of blue expanded to include dots that they had previously excluded. The experiment was repeated with more complex scenarios than the colour of a dot, such as aggression and unethical behaviour.

Just as with the blue dots, participants saw occurrences of these in instances which they didn't see them before. The researchers concluded that:

> Although modern societies have made extraordinary progress... the majority of people believe that the world is getting worse. The fact that concepts grow larger when their instances grow smaller may be one source of that pessimism. [127]

In a similar way, employees might expand their concept of adversity as fewer instances of it occur in the workplace. This could derail attempts of aspiring to ever more comfortable environments and polished experiences in the workplace as employees might just find adversity where they didn't experience it before. If we can't get rid of adversity, at least we could explore how to make the most out of it.

We will conclude our chase of Signpost 4 with a chat with Dr. Natasha Layton. When Natasha and I meet for coffee, she would say: "let's get the environment right!" and proceed to move the chairs and table to ensure that we are both sitting comfortably, without glare or any other environmental discomfort. Natasha is not an architect nor an interior designer and moves things around with disregard to the design intent, but with the conviction of an occupational therapist. Natasha studies the relationship between person, task, and environment and consults for the World Health Organisation (WHO).

Natasha's view of the world, her knowledge map, is different from the one I depicted in Fig. 35.2. Hers is based on the WHO International Classification of Functioning (WHO-ICF) [128], a classification of human endeavours with an incredibly comprehensive list of factors that we interact with in the course of our daily life. This framework includes environmental factors like temperature and light as well as a variety of intangible factors such as attitudes and 'support and relationships'. One thing that all these have in common, Natasha explained to me, is that they are all neutral. These factors can be either a barrier or a facilitator depending on the individual, the task, and the desired outcome.

In other words, there is no objective adversity as such, it depends on the circumstances. "What I aim for is to remove all the barriers and create a lot of facilitators for excellent functioning", Natasha added. At this point I hesitate to ask if she thought adversity was a good thing, but I soldier on:

> Oh, yes, but health practitioners would call it 'treatment planning'. We increase the amount of challenge that the environment asks from the person to increase physical and cognitive functions to prepare them for a workplace.

Her answer gave me courage to ask what type of adversity she would prescribe in a workplace to promote innovation:

> If I were to implement an adversity, to use your word, I would do so with a goal in mind. The innovation that I would like to see the most in any workplace is an appreciation of what it means to be human and what comes with that is a gratitude around working.

Natasha then told me of her experience consulting for another large organisation which hires experts with lived experience of disability: "the accommodations needed in a workplace that works for 'all' can actually raise challenges to work there as a non-disabled person."

Beyond ramps and accessible lunchrooms for physical access, she described the many ways in which communication must change to include people with visual and hearing impairment, and how standard communication would not work – at all. "So initially it's awkward, and you feel that it slows you down in your work, but... Oh. My. Goodness!", Natasha's face lights up with a big smile:

> When everyone can join in and you have successful interactions then, at that workplace, you can feel a profound societal shift towards inclusion. If you understand disability, you understand diversity, you understand humans.

My idea of innovation is close to Natasha's, yours might be too, or not. But what the trails of adversity suggest is that working in tangible and intangible environments which increase in just the right amount the challenge that the environment asks from the person might lead to the innovation you seek.

Open Access This chapter is licensed under the terms of the Creative Commons Attribution 4.0 International License (http://creativecommons.org/licenses/by/4.0/), which permits use, sharing, adaptation, distribution and reproduction in any medium or format, as long as you give appropriate credit to the original author(s) and the source, provide a link to the Creative Commons license and indicate if changes were made.

The images or other third party material in this chapter are included in the chapter's Creative Commons license, unless indicated otherwise in a credit line to the material. If material is not included in the chapter's Creative Commons license and your intended use is not permitted by statutory regulation or exceeds the permitted use, you will need to obtain permission directly from the copyright holder.

Chapter 36
All Roads Lead to Rome

Following Signposts takes us through trails that expose us to unique ways of viewing work, the workplace, and ourselves. However, the process can be overwhelming, and that worried Frank too:

> An organisation can only make so many changes at once, right? So, if there are 34 things that they need to do, they're going to be overwhelmed. Organisations should choose just two or three signposts, the ones which would have the most impact, and take it from there.

However, these signposts are not individual directives on workplace improvements. A confusion which comes from assuming they will take us to 34 different places. Yet, if these markers are to deliver on their promise, they would have to converge in a single destination: a better place to work, Fig. 36.1. Consequently, it is not necessary to follow them all.

Figure 36.1 also illustrates the crisscrossing of paths as we travel towards their shared destination. The vertical watermark shows, if only conceptually, how far this guide has taken us.

Signposts Converging

2020 marked Beethoven's 250 birthday; orchestras around the world paid tribute to his work which is still regarded as imaginative, uncompromising, and unprecedented [129].

Arthur Brooks, a trained musician and professor at the Harvard Kennedy School, tells us that as the hearing of the classical composer deteriorated, he was influenced less by the prevailing compositional fashions and more by the musical structures forming inside his own head [130]. Beethoven *"no longer had society's soundtrack in his ears"*, Brooks writes. Then, as Beethoven's condition worsened, he avoided frequencies he could not hear [131].

Applying our signposts to Beethoven's situation, was it the isolation that led to his unique style (Signpost 1), or was this due to adversity from losing his hearing (Signpost 4)? Perhaps he was following Signpost 2 and had broken with the rules of composition.

The example illustrates how signposts might converge at the destination rendering them undistinguishable from each other.

Fig. 36.1 Convergence of Signposts

Since I'm yet to arrive at the signposts' destination, I can only speculate about what happens there. So, I will briefly indulge in such pleasure and say that it might not be boring, uncomfortable, absurd, inefficient, and isolated – as some signpost may lead us to believe. At least not for long periods at a time. To explain, let's take a leaf out of the book of the sit-to-stand inquiries into the optimal posture to work.

After labelling sitting *"the new smoking"* [132], it turned out that similar to the risks of prolonged sitting, so too should prolonged standing be avoided [133]. The optimal posture to work is neither sitting nor standing, but 'the next one' – alternating between the two.

In a similar way, places of work should alternate between opposite sides of the coin to avoid the downsides of prolonged exposure to just one side and benefit from the advantages of the other: absurd/rational, stimulating/boring, adverse/comfortable, connected/isolated, and so on.

Open Access This chapter is licensed under the terms of the Creative Commons Attribution 4.0 International License (http://creativecommons.org/licenses/by/4.0/), which permits use, sharing, adaptation, distribution and reproduction in any medium or format, as long as you give appropriate credit to the original author(s) and the source, provide a link to the Creative Commons license and indicate if changes were made.

The images or other third party material in this chapter are included in the chapter's Creative Commons license, unless indicated otherwise in a credit line to the material. If material is not included in the chapter's Creative Commons license and your intended use is not permitted by statutory regulation or exceeds the permitted use, you will need to obtain permission directly from the copyright holder.

Chapter 37
Getting There

I haven't forgotten about the other four signposts that I discussed with the locals and Fig. 37.1 shows their individual calibration. These will not be discussed in any detail, but I do want to share just three views which came up while discussing the process of delivering a workplace (Signpost 11).

Leo who sees the workplace from the no-nonsense pragmatism of the real estate world explained:

> [Investors] produce these assets [office buildings] for the purpose of financial gain. Most of the times, it's the antithesis of innovation and they do what is tried and tested to reduce risk and increase profit.

> **Horse Poo**
> I learnt a dazzling fact on my walk to Sydney: a bag of horse poo sold for $2 in the state of Victoria, but the same commodity cost $3 once I crossed the New South Wales border.
>
> In keeping with the absurdity of my thoughts throughout the pilgrimage, I toyed with the idea of becoming a poo merchant. Clearly there was a market and if I could move one million bags across states, I'd become a millionaire. Unfortunately, mental calculations suggested it would take me a few thousand years to carry one million bags of horse poo across states – they were heavy.
>
> Still, I understood quite well the variables behind the business plan of my short-lived career change. This came with the realisation that it is easier to plan a pathway to sell shit, than it is to implement the signposts into a workplace.

Signpost 6: Boredom can become a useful thinking tool.

Signpost 11: The process of designing a workplace can get in the way of creating an environment which meets its purpose.

Signpost 25: Work and tasks are different yet interconnected.

Signpost 30: The pursuit of efficiencies might strip work of its meaning.

Fig. 37.1 Calibration of Signposts 6, 11, 25, and 30. Established view (left), Personal view (right)

As an Architect this sentiment is never easy to hear, but I have heard it before from others in property development where the value of the building resides in its return on investment and little else.

Frank expanded on that idea from the architect's perspective:

> Mass architecture is about big buildings and big finance. We've got ourselves locked into a mindset in which only large corporations can build on our behalf… in which 'form follows finance'.

37 Getting There

I missed most of what Frank said afterwards, I was still processing 'form follows finance' – a clever, albeit disheartening, update of *'form follows function'* axiom by Louis Sullivan [134].

Thankfully, I was recording the conversation because what Frank said next was quite relevant too:

> The purpose of an architectural firm is to make architecture. So, no architectural firm will challenge whether or not you need that new workplace. And some will say that they do, but they don't, really, because there would be a loss of fee.

Indeed, it's so rare for architects to propose a non building-based solution that when they do, it becomes a TED talk. In *Architecture for the people by the people* [135], Architect Alastair Parvin argues that architecture is about solving problems, not about making buildings which he sees as just about the most expensive solution to almost any given problem. What about losing those fees? From that same talk:

> *Now, it looks like you're doing yourself out of a job, but you're not. You're actually making yourself more useful. Architects are actually really, really good at this kind of resourceful, strategic thinking. And the problem is that, like a lot of design professions, we got fixated on the idea of providing a particular kind of consumer product, and I don't think that needs to be the case anymore.* [135]

This view of architecture does not take away the product the discipline is best known for – undoubtably, there are instances in which a building, or more broadly a 'space solution', is the best answer to a problem. Instead, it expands the range of answers available to architects and designers. In his talk, you can learn how Parvin solved an architectural problem with a bell and a watch.

Last, but not least Henry who is in charge of delivering workplace solutions for a large organisation posed a rhetorical question, "why do large enterprises exists?" His stark answer:

> [Organisations] exist to drive shareholder value. The CFO's role is to count beans and the more beans they count, the better.

That is indeed a severe and abbreviated representation of large enterprises; however, one can read the works behind the 'Theory of the Firm' [136] and learn a lot about specialisation, organisational structures, employees' and employer's relationships, even about the intangibility of firms themselves and walk away with an overarching impression not too far from Henry's.

These views from just three of our locals are a good description of the context that comes into play well before designers have the opportunity to consider what happens in the workplace – or apply signposts.

Promisingly, a consistent message emerged from talking with Leo, Frank, Henry and the other locals: they wanted change. The vast majority (over 80%) of our locals would rather head closer to the signposts than the established view.

The Pilgrim's World vs the Real World
Shortly after returning from my pilgrimage I had a much anticipated lunch with a work colleague who happens to be the mastermind behind countless global workplace strategies. I looked forward to hearing my colleague's feedback about my ideas and so I shared a very early version of the still developing Signposts.

As we conversed, a subtle smile crossed my confidant's face that prefaced a question I would hear many times:

> It all sounds great! But how will you go about implementing these ideas in the real world?

The fact is, a pilgrim's world doesn't always fit in the 'real world', but that doesn't mean it can't, nor that it shouldn't.

*

In Part I of this book, I shared my motivation for walking from Melbourne to Sydney and in Part II, I took you through my preparations leading to my first step. In Parts III and IV I brought you along my analogue and virtual pilgrimages where we saw many Signposts rise. Having already completed the journey and sharing what I learned, I was just that little bit ahead of you, but in Part V you caught up with me. We met at the end of the trail and from there on, we travelled shoulder to shoulder laying paths.

In the next, and last Part, we go separate ways. However, I am hopeful we will meet again at the destination of the Signposts.

Open Access This chapter is licensed under the terms of the Creative Commons Attribution 4.0 International License (http://creativecommons.org/licenses/by/4.0/), which permits use, sharing, adaptation, distribution and reproduction in any medium or format, as long as you give appropriate credit to the original author(s) and the source, provide a link to the Creative Commons license and indicate if changes were made.

The images or other third party material in this chapter are included in the chapter's Creative Commons license, unless indicated otherwise in a credit line to the material. If material is not included in the chapter's Creative Commons license and your intended use is not permitted by statutory regulation or exceeds the permitted use, you will need to obtain permission directly from the copyright holder.

Part VI
Your Creature

Chapter 38
My Iguana, Your Creature

This book freezes my pursuit of Signposts in search of a better place to work, what I have referred to as 'my iguana'. But the ideas which underpin my creature will continue to evolve beyond the pages of this book. Not only because I will keep laying paths, but also because of you.

There might be ideas here that you agree with, and no doubt others you vehemently oppose; both a catalyst for you to create an iguana-like creature of your own.

Having travelled this journey, my advice is not to ignore the nagging thoughts that come from your creature. Instead, I encourage you to take it on a pilgrimage of your own. Walk if you feel it's necessary, or don't, but allow yourself to explore the absurd and follow your creature to a place that is beyond the beaten track.

Then lay paths to reach your version of the workplace. I hope we meet there.

Although I have more to say, I prefer to get out of your way now and wish you a "buen camino".

Open Access This chapter is licensed under the terms of the Creative Commons Attribution 4.0 International License (http://creativecommons.org/licenses/by/4.0/), which permits use, sharing, adaptation, distribution and reproduction in any medium or format, as long as you give appropriate credit to the original author(s) and the source, provide a link to the Creative Commons license and indicate if changes were made.

The images or other third party material in this chapter are included in the chapter's Creative Commons license, unless indicated otherwise in a credit line to the material. If material is not included in the chapter's Creative Commons license and your intended use is not permitted by statutory regulation or exceeds the permitted use, you will need to obtain permission directly from the copyright holder.

Acknowledgements

"You are nuts!" said Mark Bray, when I told him my idea of walking to Sydney, but he quickly added "how can I help you?" Mark was the first person I shared my plans with and if that conversation had gone any differently my pilgrimage might not have happened.

Writing this book was an equally crazy idea for which I will be forever grateful to Dr. Peter Edwards, Laurie Aznavoorian, and Prue Vincent for their encouragement, editing and helping me find a voice to communicate the absurdities of this book.

I also acknowledge the dedication of a group of readers of early drafts of the manuscript whose feedback helped to keep the content relevant to a wide readership: Dr. Natasha Layton, Hannah Bauer, Dr. Lina Engelen, Marilyn Zakhour, Brian Stevenson, Paul Turner, Dr. Patricia Chevez-Barrios, Cai Kjaer, Daniel Davis, Iulia Istrate, Evodia Alaterou, Kate Torkington, Katie Puckett, and Mark Vender. I am also extremely grateful to the anonymous peer reviewers.

In the References section I have cited the people and organisations around the world with whom I have enjoyed opportunities to do research.

The artwork illustrating this book is from Sam Jenkins who managed to beautifully communicate the essence behind each illustration.

Thank you to Kerry and Cynthia Turner and all the other locals I encountered during my walk to Sydney. And, of course, to the 22 anonymous 'locals' who got me closer to where the Signposts point.

Genevieve McNamara, thank you for the pillow which made me wonder about comfort in the workplace, and Dr. Michelle Turner for the trusty pair of socks and support throughout the walking and writing. To my family and friends, thank you all.

Finally, I want to acknowledge Lucie Bartonek, Springer's editor who saw potential in a book about the workplace with unusual headings.

Appendices

Appendix A: List of Signposts

1. Exchanging ideas too early and too often hinders their diversity and potential to innovate.
2. The workplace should promote absurdity.
3. The workplace should nurture our human traits.
4. Adversities are worth keeping, even introduced, in the workplace to promote innovation.
5. Aloneness needs to be within the ideal conditions of its effects on us (solitude) and the quality of the idea itself.
6. Boredom can become a useful thinking tool.
7. The subjectivity behind preparedness and readiness hinders the benchmarking of workplaces.
8. Understanding the meaning of the workplace as well as its function can lead to better places of work.
9. Experience design and organisation design need to be aligned in the workplace for the organisation to achieve its objectives.
10. Moving at slow speed allows us to interact with people, but we still need symbols in the workplace for others and for our personal identity.
11. The process of designing a workplace can get in the way of creating an environment which meets its purpose.
12. There is beauty in the ugliness of personalisation.
13. Absurdity can result in greater meaning and purpose.
14. Seeing normality through absurdity can show the absurd as normal.
15. Normality can be the offspring of the unchallenged.
16. Strong cohesion can have the benefits and pitfalls of a small country town.
17. Increasing opportunities to socialise might not result in a more inclusive environment.
18. The noise of knowledge transfer could be the sound of collaboration.

19. Designing work first and then the workplace could lead to dramatic new forms of value.
20. Good design aligns the work aesthetic of an organisation with its looks.
21. Social proximity can promote empathy.
22. (B)ehaviour in the workplace can vary as a result of changes in the (E)nvironment and/or the (P)erson.
23. The workplace is not only what we can measure.
24. The difficulty in changing our beliefs can hinder the adoption of innovation.
25. Work and tasks are different yet interconnected.
26. Work is intangible, tasks are tangible.
27. Work is more than its output.
28. The workplace could benefit from lessons derived from instances where work can't be done.
29. Work which is aligned with its environment does not require added meaning.
30. The pursuit of efficiencies might strip work of its meaning.
31. The need of gamification and added rituals might be tell-tale signs of an overly efficient workplace.
32. Understanding work cues can help improve current and emerging work environments.
33. The workplace is also what it is not.
34. In the absence of work, with only tasks left to do, no workplace would suffice.

Appendix B: Meet the Locals (Table 1)

Table 1 Signpost locals

Pseudonym	Position description
Alice (f)	PhD candidate on organisational culture and creativity
Brooke (f)	Workplace design leader at architecture firm
Claire (f)	Chief Strategy Officer at communications agency
David (m)	Multi-disciplinary designer at own practice
Ethan (m)	Management researcher at university
Frank (m)	Researcher at architecture firm
Gavin (m)	Design historian at university
Henry (m)	Director of workplace solutions at large organisation
Isabel (f)	Workplace strategist at global technology and property organisation
Julia (f)	Founder of boutique consultancy on distributed teams
Kevin (m)	Workplace strategist at global corporate real estate service provider
Leo (m)	Director at property advisory and project management firm
Miles (m)	Postdoctoral organisation design researcher at business school
Nora (f)	Consultant at a workplace strategy and change management consultancy

(continued)

Appendices

Table 1 (continued)

Pseudonym	Position description
Olivia (f)	Director at global experience design consultancy
Paula (f)	Futurist at architecture firm
Quinn (f)	Flexible workplace consultant
Ron (m)	Industry observer of cutting-edge workplaces at design firm
Sarah (f)	Remote work and future of work consultant
Talia (f)	Design strategist at architecture firm
Uriel (m)	Workplace technology consultant
Vincent (m)	Workplace designer at architecture firm

A gender balanced viewpoint was sought across interviewees, 50% are females. Their pseudonyms indicate gender: (f)emale/(m)ale

Appendix C: Signpost Calibration (Table 2)

Table 2 Distribution of results of calibrations

Signpost		Opposite way	Ignore	That way, but not there	Go there	Total
1: Exchange of Ideas	P	**9%** (2)	–	**77%** (17)	**14%** (3)	**100%** (22)
	E	**59%** (13)	**27%** (6)	**14%** (3)	–	**100%** (22)
2: Absurdity	P	–	**5%** (1)	**36%** (8)	**59%** (13)	**100%** (22)
	E	**41%** (9)	**14%** (3)	**41%** (9)	**5%** (1)	**100%** (22)
4.1: Adversity (Keep)	P	**14%** (3)	**14%** (3)	**36%** (8)	**36%** (8)	**100%** (22)
	E	**73%** (16)	**18%** (4)	**9%** (2)	–	**100%** (22)
4.2: Adversity (Introduce)	P	**9%** (2)	**9%** (2)	**27%** (6)	**55%** (12)	**100%** (22)
	E	**64%** (14)	**23%** (5)	**14%** (3)	–	**100%** (22)
6: Boredom	P	–	–	**18%** (4)	**82%** (18)	**100%** (22)
	E	**41%** (9)	**36%** (8)	**18%** (4)	**5%** (1)	**100%** (22)
11: Process vs Purpose	P	–	**14%** (3)	**23%** (5)	**64%** (14)	**100%** (22)
	E	**36%** (8)	**45%** (10)	**18%** (4)	–	**100%** (22)
25: Work vs Tasks	P	–	–	**18%** (4)	**82%** (18)	**100%** (22)
	E	**23%** (5)	**23%** (5)	**27%** (6)	**27%** (6)	**100%** (22)
30: Efficiency vs Meaning	P	**5%** (1)	–	**32%** (7)	**64%** (14)	**100%** (22)
	E	**45%** (10)	**27%** (6)	**23%** (5)	**5%** (1)	**100%** (22)
Total	P	**5%** (8)	**5%** (9)	**34%** (59)	**57%** (100)	**100%** (176)
	E	**48%** (84)	**27%** (47)	**20%** (36)	**5%** (9)	**100%** (176)

(P)ersonal, **(E)**stablished | **Percentage**% (frequency)

References

1. Chevez A (2009) Evolution of workplace architecture as a consequence of technology development. RMIT University, Melbourne
2. Dawkins R (2012) The magic of reality. Black Swan
3. Chevez A (2018) The benefits – and pitfalls – of working in isolation. The Conversation, 9 Novembre 2018
4. O'Neill N (2018) Antarctica scientist stabbed colleague for spoiling book endings. New York Post , 30 October 2018
5. Leavitt J, Christenfeld N (2011) Story spoilers don't spoil stories. Psychol Sci 22(9):1152–1154
6. Prime Minister of Australia (2020) Transcript, Address National Press Club, 26 May 2020. [Online]. Available: https://www.pm.gov.au/media/address-national-press-club-260520. Accessed 10 July 2020
7. Salmon W (1980) A contemporary look at Zeno's paradoxes. In: Space, time and motion. University of Minnesota Press, Minneapolis
8. Descartes R (1984) Principles of philosophy, vol 24. Springer Science & Business Media, Cham
9. Huber T, Rigzin T (1995) A Tibetan guide for pilgrimage to Ti-se (Mount Kailas) and mTsho Ma-phatn (Lake Manasarovar). Tibet J 20(1):10–47
10. Shilling C, Mellor P (2010) Saved from pain or saved through pain? Modernity, instrumentalization and the religious use of pain as a body technique. Eur J Soc Theory 13(4):521–537
11. Reed C, Director (1949) The Third Man. [Film]. London Films
12. Clements-Croome D (2006) Creating the productive workplace. Taylor & Francis, London
13. Barker S, Grayhem P, Koon J, Perkins J, Whalen A, Raudenbush B (2003) Improved performance on clerical tasks associated with administration of peppermint odor. Percept Mot Skills:1007–1010
14. Kidd IJ (2018) Adversity, wisdom, and exemplarism. J Value Inq 52(4):379–393
15. Ludwig A (1998) Method and madness in the arts and sciences. Creat Res J 11(2):93–101
16. Nietzsche F (2008) Thus spoke Zarathustra. Oxford University Press, Oxford
17. Niehues A, Broom A, Tranter P, Ragen J, Engelen L (2013) Everyday uncertainties: reframing perceptions of risk in outdoor free play. J Advent Educ Outdoor Learn 13(3):223–237
18. Rose L (2016) The human side of virtual work: managing trust, isolation, and presence, 1st edn. Business Expert Press, New York
19. Murthy V (2017) Work and the loneliness epidemic. Harvard Business Review, 26 September 2017
20. Pentland A (2013) Beyond the echo chamber. Harvard Business Review, November 2013
21. Wilson T, Reinhard D, Westgate E, Gilbert D, Ellerbeck N, Hahn C, Brown C, Shaked A (2014) Just think: the challenges of the disengaged mind. Science 345(6192):75–77
22. Herzog W (2014) Of walking in ice. Penguin, Paris

23. Chevez A, Gladwish L (2018) Exploring what's next in Corporate Real Estate: filling the void: a post coworking environment. Pepper Property, Melbourne
24. Pilgrim P (1998) Peace pilgrim: her life and work in her own words, 2nd edn. Ocean Tree Books, Shelton
25. van der Zande J, Teigland K, Siri S, Teigland R (2018) The substitution of labor: from technological feasibility to other factors influencing job automation. Center for Strategy and Competitiveness, Stockolm
26. Morse NC, Weiss RS (1955) The function and meaning of work and the job. Am Sociol Rev 20(2):191–198
27. Rosso BD, Dekas KH, Wrzesniewski A (2010) On the meaning of work: a theoretical integration and review. Res Organ Behav 30:91–127
28. McLellan H (2000) Experience design. CyberPsychol Behav 3(1):59–69
29. Puranam P, Chevez A (2019) When is cool office design more than window dressing? INSEAD Knowledge, 23 August 2019
30. Venturi R, Scott Brown D, Izenour S (1972) Learning from Las Vegas. MIT Press, Cambridge
31. Ashkanasy NM, Ayoko OB, Jehn KA (2014) Understanding the physical environment of work and employee behavior: an affective events perspective. J Organ Behav:1169–1184
32. Morricone E, Composer (1966) The good, the bad and the ugly. [Sound Recording]. Capitol Records
33. Pryke S (2008) Social network analysis. In: Advanced research methods in the built environment. Wiley-Blackwell, New York, pp 171–182
34. Guthrum. Power nap comic. [Online]. Available: http://www.powernapcomic.com/. Accessed 10 June 2021
35. Terwiesch C (2019) Empirical research in operations management: from field studies to analyzing digital exhaust. Manuf Serv Oper Manag 21(4):713–722
36. Galindo-Romero M, Yi Fong K, Chevez A (2019) The sound of collaboration in open-plan offices: a pilot study. In: INTER-NOISE and NOISE-CON Congress and conference proceedings, vol 259, no 2
37. Bernstein E, Turban S (2018) The impact of the 'open' workspace on human collaboration. Philos Trans R Soc B Biol Sci 373(1753):1–8
38. Groves D (2009) Crime and architecture: designing a Centre for Australian Crime Fiction. Latrobe J 83:13–27
39. Brown T (2008) Design thinking. Harvard Business Review, June 2008
40. Zemeckis R (1994) Director, Forrest Gump. [Film]. Paramount Pictures Studios
41. Lewin K (1936) Principles of topological psychology. McGraw-Hill Publications in Psychology, New York
42. Bechtel R (1977) Enclosing behaviour. Dowden Hutchinson & Ross, Stroudsberg
43. Kihlstrom J (2013) The person-situation interaction. In: The Oxford handbook of social cognition. Oxford University Press, Oxford, pp 786–805
44. Kelly P, Carmody K, Composers (1993) From little things, big things grow. [Sound Recording]. Festival
45. Thomas B, Kristen L (2019) Development and validation of the workplace dignity scale. Group Org Manag 44(1):72–111
46. Chevez A, Simpson K, Bauer H, Wohlgezogen F, Maak T, Thomas B, Kjaer C (2019) Designing for dignity. HASSELL
47. Cameron WB (1963) Informal Sociology, a casual introduction to sociological thinking. Random House, New York, p 13
48. Bagehot W (1872), Physics and politics. BoD-Books on Demand (re-issued 2019)
49. Rogers EM (2010) Diffusion of innovations. Simon and Schuster
50. Whiteford G (1997) Occupational deprivation and incarceration. J Occup Sci 4(3):126–130
51. Whiteford G (2000) Occupational deprivation: global challenge in the new millennium. Br J Occup Ther 63(5):200–204
52. Christie A (1934) Murder on the orient express. Collins Crime Club, London

References

53. Coelho P (1987) The pilgrimage. Harper Collins, New York
54. Estevez E, Director (2010) The way. [Film]. Filmax
55. Smith LB, Director (2015) Walking the Camino: six ways to Santiago. [Film]. Lydia B. Smith, Sally Bentley, Theresa Tollini-Coleman
56. Visit Colorado Springs. The Manitou Incline [Online]. Available: https://www.visitcos.com/things-to-do/outdoors/manitou-incline-near-colorado-springs-colorado/. Accessed 2 Apr 2021
57. Monaghan S (2020) These two (friendly) rivals are setting insane Manitou incline records. [Online]. Available: https://www.5280.com/2019/12/these-two-friendly-rivals-are-setting-insane-manitou-incline-records/. Accessed 2 Apr 2021
58. Peat C (2021) Heavens above: ISS – Orbit. [Online]. Available: https://www.heavens-above.com/orbit.aspx?satid=25544. Accessed 2 Apr 2021
59. Centrical (2021) [Online]. Available: https://centrical.com/platform/gamification/. Accessed 2 Apr 2021
60. Weber M, Kalberg S (2013) The protestant ethic and the spirit of capitalism. Routledge
61. Cosmic Centaurs. Rituals. [Online]. Available: https://www.cosmiccentaurs.com/ritual-bank. Accessed 2 Apr 2021
62. Weber M (2013) From Max Weber: essays in sociology. Routledge, London
63. Taylor F (2004) Scientific management. Routledge, London
64. Bartle R (2004) Designing virtual worlds. New Riders, London
65. Cicognani A (2003) Architectural design for online environments. In: Virtual publics: policy and community in an electronic age. Columbia University Press, New York, pp 83–111
66. Davis N (2012) Digital apocalypse: living through the death of virtual worlds. The Verge, 20 December 2012. [Online]. Available: https://www.theverge.com/2012/12/20/3776210/electric-funeral-death-of-mmo. Accessed 2 Apr 2021
67. Second Life (2021) Remote work and event solutions. Linden Research. [Online]. Available: https://www.connect.secondlife.com/. Accessed 2 Apr 2021
68. Dean G (2021) Mark Zuckerberg snuck sunscreen, Sweet Baby Ray's BBQ sauce, and other props poking fun at his past into Facebook's 'Meta' rebrand. Business Insider, 29 October 2021
69. Call in Colonel Mustard For Questioning. [Sound Recording]. This American Life
70. James P, Veit WF, Wright SJ (1997) Work of the future: global perspectives. Allen & Unwin, New York
71. Clark SC (2000) Work/family border theory: a new theory of work/family balance. Hum Relat 53(6):747–770
72. Chevez A, Huppatz DJ (2017) A short history of the office. The Conversation, 14 August 2017
73. Rybczynski W (1987) Home: a short history of an idea. Penguin
74. Godden DR, Baddeley AD (1975) Context-dependent memory in two natural environments: land and underwater. Br J Psychol 66:325–331
75. Chevez A (2017) What workspaces are the best for freelance workers? The Conversation, 24 January 2017
76. Smith S, Vela E (2001) Environmental context-dependent memory: a review and meta-analysis. Psychon Bull Rev 8(2):203–220
77. Frankl V (1985) Man's search for meaning. Simon and Schuster, London
78. Moor R (2016) On trails. Aurum Press, New York
79. Zheng N-n, Liu Z-y, Ren P-j, Ma Y-q, Chen S-t, Yu S-y, Xue J-r, Chen B-d, Wang F-y (2017) Hybrid-augmented intelligence: collaboration and cognition. Front Inf Technol Electron Eng 18(2):153–179
80. Life as a pilgrim. [Film]. All Saints Church Passadena
81. Cronon W (1996) The trouble with wilderness: or, getting back to the wrong nature. Environ Hist 1(1):7–28
82. Oxford reference. Carnivalesque. [Online]. Available: https://www.oxfordreference.com/view/10.1093/oi/authority.20110803095550811. Accessed 11 Oct 2021
83. Bakhtin M (2013) Problems of Dostoevsky's poetics, vol 8. University of Minnesota Press, Minneapolis

84. Vohs KD, Redden JP, Rahinel R (2013) Physical order produces healthy choices, generosity, and conventionality, whereas disorder produces creativity. Psychol Sci 24(9):1860–1867
85. Hopkins O (2020) Postmodern architecture: less is a bore. Phaidon Press, London
86. March J (2020) The technology of foolishness. In: Shaping entrepreneurship research. Routledge, Abingdon, pp 120–130
87. Larsen B (2020) Whatever happened to "The Technology of Foolishness"? Does it have any potential today? Scand J Manag 36(1)
88. Farson R (1997) Management of the absurd. Simon and Schuster, New York
89. Johansen JH (2018) Paradox management: contradictions and tensions in complex organizations. Springer, Cham
90. Camus A (2013) The myth of Sisyphus. Penguin, New York
91. Thomas E (2012) In search of Lost Art: Kurt Schwitters's Merzbau. MoMA. [Online]. Available: https://www.moma.org/explore/inside_out/2012/07/09/in-search-of-lost-art-kurt-schwitterss-merzbau/. Accessed 15 Jan 2022
92. Grossman ML (1968) The language of dada. J Commun 18(1):4–10
93. Foucault M (2005) Madness and civilisation: a history of insanity in the age of reason. Routledge, London
94. Andrews M (2019) Bar talk: informal social interactions, alcohol prohibition, and invention. Alcohol Prohibition, and Invention
95. Bernstein E, Shore J, Lazer D (2018) How intermittent breaks in interaction improve collective intelligence. Proc Natl Acad Sci 115(35):8734–8739
96. Elsbach KD, Pratt M (2007) The physical environment in organizations. Acad Manag Ann 1(1):181–224
97. Cross R, Rebele R, Grant A (2016) Collaborative overload. Harv Bus Rev 94(1):74–79
98. Bolino MC, William TH (2003) Going the extra mile: cultivating and managing employee citizenship behavior. Acad Manag Perspect 17(3):60–71
99. Furnham A (2000) The brainstorming myth. Bus Strategy 11(4):21–28
100. Cain S (2013) Quiet: The power of introverts in a world that can't stop talking. Broadway Books, New York
101. Steelcase. Susan Cain quiet spaces. [Online]. Available: https://www.steelcase.com/quiet-spaces/#quiet-spaces_be-me. Accessed 10 Nov 2021
102. Bacon F (1986) On adversity. In: The essays (Penguin classics). Penguin, London
103. Gordon J (2000) Creating knowledge maps by exploiting dependent relationships. In: Applications and innovations in intelligent systems VII, pp 64–78
104. Eppler M (2001) Making knowledge visible through intranet knowledge maps: concepts, elements, cases. In: Proceedings of the 34th annual Hawaii international conference on system sciences, Hawaii
105. Web of Science (2022) Clarivate. [Online]. Available: https://clarivate.com/webofsciencegroup/solutions/web-of-science/
106. Google Scholar. Google. [Online]. Available: https://scholar.google.com/
107. Open Knowledge Maps. [Online]. Available: https://openknowledgemaps.org/
108. De Clercq D, Belausteguigoitia I (2019) Coping and laughing in the face of broken promises: implications for creative behavior. Pers Rev
109. Barrett JD, Vessey WB, Griffith JA, Mracek D, Mumford M (2014) Predicting scientific creativity: the role of adversity, collaborations, and work strategies. Creat Res J 26(1):39–52
110. Pepler R, Warner R (1968) Temperature and learning: an experimental study. ASHRAE Trans 74:211–219
111. Norman D (2013) The design of everyday things. Basic Books, New York
112. Marsh P, French S (2020) The GSK workspace performance hub: promoting productivity and wellbeing through office design. Corp Real Estate J 9(4):345–360
113. Office + SpaceIQ (2021) Frictionless workplace. [Online]. Available: https://spaceiq.com/glossary/frictionless-workplace/. Accessed 10 Oct 2021

114. Rosenberger R (2020) On hostile design: theoretical and empirical prospects. Urban Stud 57(4):883–893
115. Dunne A, Raby F (2001) Design noir: the secret life of electronic objects. Springer Science & Business Media, Cham
116. Geiger SW, Cashen LH (2002) A multidimensional examination of slack and its impact on innovation. J Manag Issues 14(1):68–84
117. Leitner J, Meyer M (2013) Organizational slack and innovation. In: Encyclopedia of creativity, invention, innovation and entrepreneurship. Springer Science+ Business Media BV, Cham, pp 1412–1419
118. Katila R, Shane S (2005) When does lack of resources make new firms innovative? Acad Manag J 48(5):814–829
119. Lawton MP, Nahemow L (1973) Ecology and the aging process. In: The psychology of adult development and aging. American Psychological Association, Washington, DC, pp 619–674
120. Helson H (1964) Adaptation level theory. Harper & Row, New York
121. Ivy R, Stephens S (2003) Challenging norms: Eisenman's obsession. Architectural Record. [Online]. Available: http://archrecord.construction.com/people/interviews/archives/0310Eisenman-1.asp
122. Mellen J, MacPhee MS (2001) Philosophy of environmental enrichment: past, present, and future. Zoo Biol 20(3):211–226
123. Easter M (2021) The comfort crisis: embrace discomfort to reclaim your wild, happy, healthy self. Rodale Books, New York
124. Goggins D (2018) Can't hurt me: master your mind and defy the odds. Lion Crest
125. Deloitte. Staying fit for competition in body and mind. [Online]. Available: https://www2.deloitte.com/global/en/pages/about-deloitte/articles/athlete-resilience-marcus-elliott.html. Accessed 10 Oct 2021
126. Bandura A, Adams NE (1977) Analysis of self-efficacy theory of behavioral change. Cogn Ther Res 1(4):287–310
127. Levari DE, Gilbert DT, Wilson TD, Sievers B, Amodio D, Wheatley T (2018) Prevalence-induced concept change in human judgment. Science 360(6396):1465–1467
128. World Health Organization (2018) International classification of functioning, disability and health. [Online]. Available: https://www.who.int/standards/classifications/international-classification-of-functioning-disability-and-health. Accessed 10 Jan 2022
129. Burkholder E (2020) Three Ways Beethoven Revolutionized Music. Calgary Philharmonic Orchestra. [Online]. Available: https://calgaryphil.com/three-ways-beethoven-revolutionized-music/
130. Brooks A (2019) This holiday season, we can all learn a lesson from Beethoven. The Washington Post. [Online]. Available: https://www.washingtonpost.com/opinions/this-holiday-season-we-can-all-learn-a-lesson-from-beethoven/2019/12/13/71f21aba-1d0e-11ea-b4c1-fd0d91b60d9e_story.html. Accessed 10 Oct 2021
131. Edoardo S, Smilde AK, Saris WH (2011) Beethoven's deafness and his three styles. BMJ
132. Vallance JK, Gardiner PA, Lynch BM, D'Silva A, Boyle T, Taylor LM, Owen N (2018) Evaluating the evidence on sitting, smoking, and health: is sitting really the new smoking? Am J Public Health 108(11):1478–1482
133. Buckley JP, Hedge A, Yates T, Copeland RJ, Loosemore M, Hamer M, Bradley G, Dunstan DW (2015) The sedentary office: a growing case for change towards better health and productivity. Expert statement commissioned by Public Health England. BJSM:1–2
134. Sullivan LH (1896) The tall office building artistically considered. Lippincott's Magaz:404–409
135. Parvin A (2013) Architecture for the people by the people. [Online]. Available: https://www.ted.com/talks/alastair_parvin_architecture_for_the_people_by_the_people. Accessed 10 Oct 2020
136. Ramrattan L (2008) Review: theories of the firm by Demetri Kantarelis. Am Econ 52:117–120

The manufacturer's authorised representative in the EU is Springer Nature Customer Service Centre GmbH, Europaplatz 3, 69115 Heidelberg, Germany. If you have any concerns regarding our products, please contact ProductSafety@springernature.com

Printed and bound by CPI Group (UK) Ltd, Croydon, CR0 4YY
25/03/2026
02078170-0016